OCT – – 2014

THE BASICS OF
LIGHT

THE BASICS OF LIGHT

JOHN O. E. CLARK

ROSEN
PUBLISHING®

New York

This edition published in 2015 by:

The Rosen Publishing Group, Inc.
29 East 21st Street
New York, NY 10010

Additional end matter copyright © 2015 by The Rosen Publishing Group, Inc.

Library of Congress Cataloging-in-Publication Data

Clark, John O. E.
The basics of light/by John O. E. Clark.
    p. cm.—(Core concepts)
Includes bibliographic references and index.
ISBN 978-1-4777-7762-6 (library binding)
1. Light—Juvenile literature. I. Clark, John Owen Edward. II. Title.
QC360.C54 2015
535—d23

Manufactured in the United States of America

© 2004 Brown Bear Books Ltd.

CONTENTS

CHAPTER ONE

WHAT IS LIGHT?

Light is a type of radiation—the only type that we can see. It is produced whenever anything gets very hot, for example, in a candle flame or an electric bulb's filament. There are also cold sources of light, such as a fluorescent tube or a firefly.

Flames from a burning fuel such as wax or oil provided people with their earliest sources of light. Candles are made simply by surrounding a stringlike wick with a cylinder of wax. The heat of the flame melts the wax next to the wick, and the wax burns to produce light. An oil lamp also has a wick that dips into a reservoir of oil such as kerosene. In both the candle and the oil lamp the burning of the fuel is an example of combustion— a chemical reaction in which the fuel combines with oxygen, giving out heat and light in the process.

The first major improvement on wicks came with gas lighting, using flammable coal gas. This gas normally burns with a yellow, smoky flame.

But by introducing air and adding a mantle, a white light is produced. The mantle is a mesh coated with the oxides of various rare metals, which become incandescent—emitting a bright light— when they are heated by the gas flame.

CREATING ELECTRIC LIGHT

The earliest form of electric light was the arc light. Developed by the English scientist Humphry Davy in 1808, it consists of two carbon rods, called electrodes, with their ends a short distance apart. When the electrodes are connected to a high-voltage supply, a very bright spark (called an arc) forms between the electrodes. Modern arc lights, which may have metal electrodes, are used in movie projectors and searchlights.

When an electric current passes along a piece of thin wire, the wire gets hot. It may get red hot and even white hot before it melts or burns away. In the 1870s inventors in the United States and Great Britain tried to find ways of making an electric bulb with a filament that would get white hot without it burning away.

In 1879 Thomas Edison in the United States and Joseph Swan in Britain independently produced incandescent electric bulbs. As a filament they used a thin carbon fiber enclosed in a glass vessel from which all the air had been pumped out. Modern bulbs have a thin piece of tungsten wire as a filament and contain an inert gas—one that does not react chemically—such as argon, rather than a vacuum.

ELECTRIC LIGHT

In the arc light, the earliest type of electric light, a high-voltage spark passed between a pair of carbon electrodes. In a modern incandescent bulb the electric current heats a tungsten filament until it becomes white hot. In a fluorescent tube the main light comes from a phosphor that glows when illuminated by the blue-green light produced by an electric current flowing through mercury vapor.

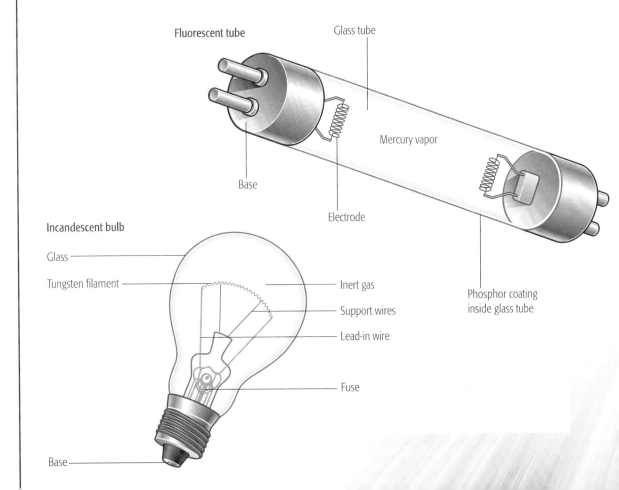

Fluorescent tube

Glass tube

Mercury vapor

Base

Electrode

Phosphor coating inside glass tube

Incandescent bulb

Glass

Tungsten filament

Inert gas

Support wires

Lead-in wire

Fuse

Base

LIGHT AND GAS

Toward the end of the 19th century scientists experimented with passing electricity through gases. Metal electrodes carried current to and from a glass tube containing gas at low pressure. Neon gas, for example, produces a bright orange light, as used in advertising signs. Mercury vapor produces a blue-green light. The inside of a modern fluorescent tube is coated with a phosphor, which gives off white light when illuminated by a mercury-vapor light inside it.

In the natural world some animals and plants produce light. Fireflies (which are actually beetles) and glowworms (beetle larvae) are familiar examples, and there are some deep-sea fish that emit light to attract their prey in the blackness of the ocean bottom. This type of light production is known as bioluminescence.

A firefly—also called a lightning bug—is a type of beetle that produces a flashing light from its abdomen. Different species flash at different rates so that they can recognize one another. The light is produced by a chemical process within the bug's body.

Scientists are studying how proteins from bioluminescent crystal jellyfish can be injected into humans to detect cancer cells.

CHAPTER TWO

CONVERTING ENERGY

All forms of energy can be converted into one another. We saw on the previous pages that chemical reactions and electricity can produce light. Here we look at how light can be changed into other forms of energy, thus enabling plants to grow, and also producing enough electricity to power, for example, a space probe.

The major source of energy on Earth is light from the Sun. Without it no form of life could survive for long. That is

A field of growing corn soaks up the sunshine, using the energy of sunlight to convert carbon dioxide and water into sugar and oxygen. The sugar is stored in the plants, while the oxygen passes into the air.

because sunlight provides the energy for photosynthesis, the process by which green plants convert carbon dioxide (from the air) and water (from the soil) into oxygen and foods such as sugars. Animals either eat plants, or they eat other animals that eat plants. So if there were no sunlight, there would be no plants or animals.

PHOTOELECTRIC CELLS

In photosynthesis light energy is converted into chemical energy, which is then stored in sugar and other plant tissues. This is a natural, biological process. But the conversion of light into electricity involves some quite advanced physics.

The simplest form of conversion takes place in a photoelectric cell, like the type used for measuring light levels in a photographer's light meter and in some cameras. The key to a photoelectric cell is a substance, such as the semimetallic element silicon, that emits electrons when light shines on it. The electrons are collected and form an electric current. Photoelectric cells are used to turn streetlights on and off automatically (they respond to the amount of daylight) and in various types of burglar alarms.

The current produced by a single photoelectric cell is very small. For

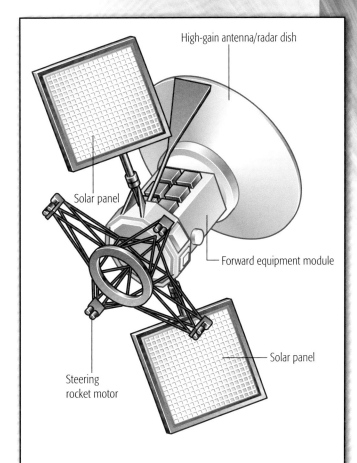

High-gain antenna/radar dish

Solar panel

Forward equipment module

Solar panel

Steering
rocket motor

Power In Space

The large "paddles" on the Magellan space probe each contained hundreds of photocells. They converted sunlight into electricity to power the probe's electronic systems.

Above: Solar panels on a roof collect the Sun's light radiation and convert it into electricity for use in the home. Below: Solar panels can be used to power vehicles, such as this car created by students at the University of Berkeley.

Satellites and probes powered by solar cells are able to absorb a lot of energy from their position in space.

larger currents hundreds of cells are constructed as panels. Large solar panels of this type are used to power the communications and control systems of space probes.

HEATING WATER

Solar panels of a different type can be seen on the roofs of some buildings. They consist of very thin, hollow panels containing water, with one of the large surfaces blackened and positioned so that it faces the Sun for most of the day. The blackened surface absorbs solar radiation and heats water that is pumped through the panel. The warmed water may be used in a heating system—it takes less extra energy to heat water that is already warm than to heat cold water.

CHAPTER THREE

THE MOVEMENT OF LIGHT

Light from a source such as the Sun or an electric lamp travels out in all directions at an incredibly high speed. It travels in straight lines. Light passes right through transparent substances such as glass and clear plastic. Substances that do not allow light to pass through them are called opaque, and opaque objects cast shadows.

Proving that light travels in straight lines is easy because it makes opaque objects in its way cast shadows. The shadows produced by a small concentrated light source have sharp edges. The shadow is the area that the rays of light from the source cannot reach.

The biggest shadow we can ever see is the shadow of the Earth itself. The Sun makes the Earth cast a long shadow into space, pointing away from the Sun. Occasionally the Moon moves into the Earth's shadow. The Moon shines by reflecting light from the Sun. But when the Earth's shadow falls on the Moon, the Moon ceases to shine. This is called an eclipse of the Moon, or a lunar eclipse.

Sometimes the Moon, moving in its orbit, passes exactly between the Earth and

This photograph was taken just before the Moon's shadow completely cut off the light from the Sun.

LUNAR AND SOLAR ECLIPSES (NOT TO SCALE)

During a solar eclipse (a) the Moon passes between the Earth and the Sun, stopping the Sun's light from reaching the Earth. During a lunar eclipse (b) the Earth blocks light from the Sun so that the light cannot reach the Moon and let it shine.

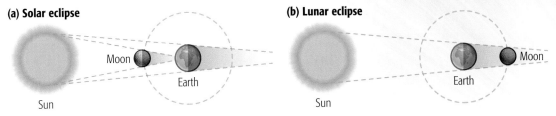

(a) Solar eclipse

Moon
Earth
Sun

(b) Lunar eclipse

Moon
Earth
Sun

TOTAL, ANNULAR, AND PARTIAL ECLIPSES (NOT TO SCALE)

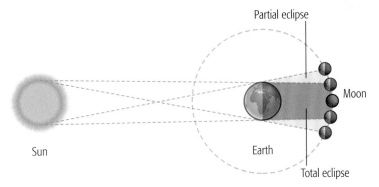

Partial eclipse

Moon

Sun

Earth

Total eclipse

As the Moon orbits the Earth, it passes into the Earth's shadow, making first a partial eclipse and then a total eclipse of the Moon.

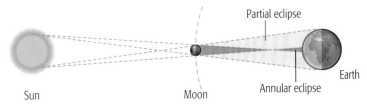

Partial eclipse

Earth

Annular eclipse

Sun

Moon

When the Moon is slightly farther away from Earth than usual, it does not completely cover the Sun's disk, and we see an annular eclipse of the Sun.

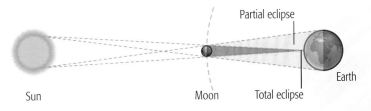

Partial eclipse

Earth

Sun

Moon

Total eclipse

With the Moon at its usual distance from Earth there is a small region where the solar eclipse is total. Elsewhere it is partial.

the Sun. A shadow of the Moon tracks across the face of the Earth. For anybody in this shadow the Moon blocks out the light of the Sun, and it becomes nearly as dark as night. This is called an eclipse of the Sun, or a solar eclipse.

Solar eclipses are important to astronomers because they allow the scientists to study the Sun's outer atmosphere, called the corona, not normally seen because the Sun is so bright. But during an eclipse the bright disk of the Sun is blocked off, and the corona shows up as a pearly swathe of light surrounding the dark Moon.

The distance between the Sun and the Moon is not always exactly the same. It varies slightly because the Moon's orbit is not perfectly regular. Sometimes the Moon does not completely block out the Sun. (The illustrations on the previous page are not to scale; the relative distances and sizes are much greater than shown.)

WAVES AND STREAMS

Light traveling along its straight path is known as a light ray. Later sections of this book explain what happens to rays

Telescopes allow professional astronomers and amateur stargazers to get a closer look at outer space.

of light when they are reflected by polished surfaces—such as mirrors—or when they pass through pieces of glass, such as lenses. A collection or bundle of light rays make up a light beam. Flashlights and searchlights produce beams of light.

Many of the properties of light can be explained by assuming that light travels as waves. For example, the wave theory of light gives a good explanation of how light is reflected by a mirror or why the colors of the rainbow can be seen in a soap bubble.

But in some situations light behaves as if it is a stream of particles, like a barrage of tiny, high-speed bullets from a machine gun. Modern physics can account for both the wave theory and the particle theory of light.

Like a rainbow in the sky, bubbles often appear with a rainbow of colors because of the way water reflects light.

CHAPTER FOUR

FINDING THE SPEED OF LIGHT

Light is the fastest thing in the universe, and nothing can move any faster. It took physicists and astronomers many years to measure the speed of light. This speed is an incredible 300,000 kilometers per second (186,000 miles per second).

When you enter a darkened room and turn on the light switch, the room seems to be flooded with light

Beams of light slice through the sky over a city as part of a laser light show. Scientists have directed a laser beam at the Moon, from where it was reflected back to Earth by a mirror left by Apollo astronauts. From a knowledge of the speed of light and the time taken for the beam to make the round trip, the Moon's distance can be found very accurately.

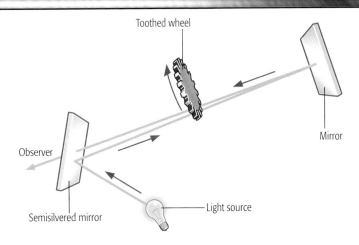

Speed of Light: Fizeau's Method

Light is reflected by a semisilvered mirror between the teeth of a fast-rotating wheel to another mirror 9 km (5.6 miles) away. The returning beam passes between the next pair of teeth and then through the semisilvered mirror to the observer. The speed of the wheel is adjusted so that there is no flicker of the light when it travels the 9 km (5.6 miles) and back.

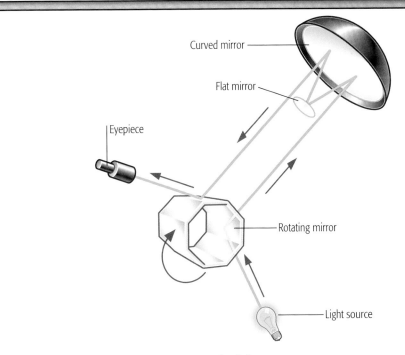

Speed of Light: Michelson's Method

A mirror on a rotating drum reflects a beam of light to a mirror 35 km (nearly 22 miles) away. The returning beam is reflected into an eyepiece. The image is steady when the drum rotates by one mirror during the round trip.

immediately. In fact, it does take a tiny instant of time for the light to reach your eyes, but light travels so fast it seems to arrive instantly.

The speed of light has been measured as 300,000 kilometers per second. At this speed it takes light reflected from the Moon only just over a second to reach the Earth. Light from the Sun has to travel about 150 million kilometers to reach the Earth, and yet it does so in just over 8 minutes.

A CHALLENGING MEASUREMENT

For many years, measuring the speed of light proved to be a great challenge to

Light travels so fast, it seems to arrive in a room instantly as soon as you turn on a lamp!

Hippolyte Fizeau made many important observations of heat and light.

scientists. The first measurement was made by the Danish astronomer Ole Römer, who in 1676 roughly estimated the speed of light by observing eclipses of Jupiter's moons. Then, in 1690 the Dutch scientist Christiaan Huygens calculated the speed as just over 230,000 kilometers a second (which is lower than the correct value by nearly 25 percent). More accurate measurements had to await the work of other scientists many years later. In 1849 the French physicist Hippolyte Fizeau used a rotating toothed wheel to measure the time it took light to make a round trip of 18 kilometers. His result was within 1 percent of the correct value. Over 30 years later the American scientist Albert Michelson increased the distance traveled by the light to 70 kilometers. He used rotating mirrors instead of a toothed wheel and obtained a value for the speed of light that was very close to the modern figure—which, to be precise, is 299,792.5 kilometers per second.

In each method the rotating wheel or mirror drum acted to interrupt the beam of light. The wheel or mirrors were rotated by an electric motor. The observer slowly increased the speed of the motor until the light did not flicker. The time taken for the light to make the round trip could then be calculated from the rotation speed of the wheel or mirrors.

REFRACTION

Light travels through air very slightly slower than it travels through a vacuum. Shining a ray of light into a rectangular block of glass slows it down even more. Its speed falls to about 200,000 kilometers a second, only two-thirds of the speed of light in vacuum.

The result of the change in speed is to make the light ray alter its direction inside the glass block. This effect is called refraction, and it will be described in detail later in the book. The slowing down is caused by the incoming light waves interacting with electrons in the atoms of the glass. As soon as the light ray leaves the glass block, it returns to its original speed and direction. In this way pieces of glass can bend light rays. This is how lenses and prisms, used in microscopes, binoculars, and other instruments, work.

Binoculars are used to make things far away appear closer.

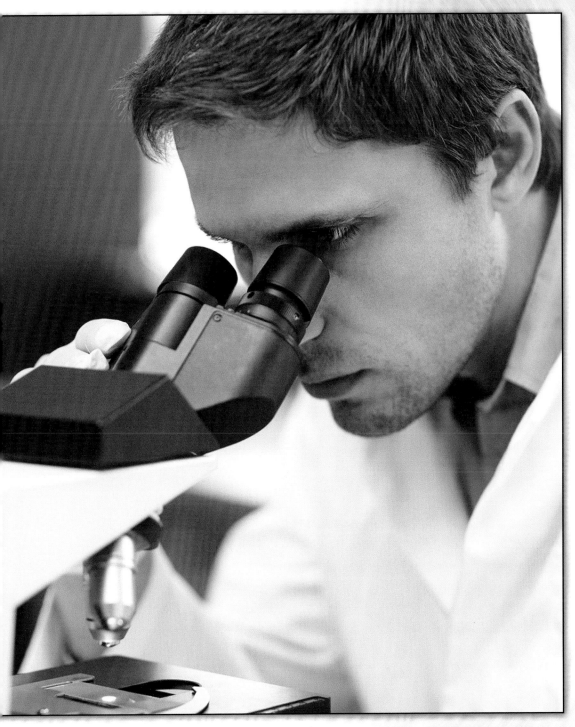

Scientists use the lenses in microscopes to see things too small for the naked eye, such as cells and bacteria.

CHAPTER FIVE

MIRRORS AND REFLECTIONS

When a ray of light strikes a flat mirror, it is reflected. It bounces off the mirror at the same angle at which it strikes it, just like a ball bouncing off the ground. Curved mirrors behave differently, depending on whether they are curved inward (concave) or outward (convex). But all types of mirrors form images of objects reflected in them.

All things reflect some of the light that falls on them. If they did not, we would not be able to see them. But the reflected light is scattered in all directions.

The windows of this building create a concave shape.

Flat, or plane, mirrors reflect nearly all of the light that falls on them, and they reflect it in the same direction.

A ray of light striking a mirror is called the incident ray. The angle at which it strikes the mirror, that is, the angle between the incident ray and a right angle to the mirror (called the normal), is known as the angle of incidence. The angle at which the light ray leaves the mirror is the angle of reflection. According to the laws of reflection of light, for a plane mirror the angle of incidence equals the angle of reflection. Also, the incident ray, the normal, and the reflected ray all lie in the same plane.

VIRTUAL IMAGES

When a mirror reflects a light ray from an object, it reaches our eyes. We then look back along the direction of the reflected ray and see an image of the object apparently behind the mirror. It is not a real image—you could not put it on a screen located behind the mirror. It is therefore known as a virtual image. An image that can be put on a screen is called a real image.

Another property of plane mirrors is that they form

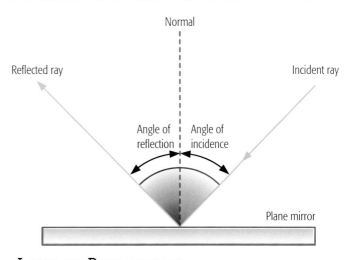

LAWS OF REFLECTION

At a plane mirror the angles of incidence and reflection are equal. The incident ray, normal, and reflected ray are in the same plane.

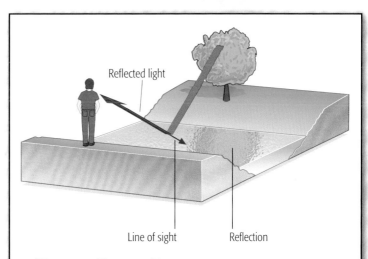

UPSIDE-DOWN TREE

The surface of the lake reflects light rays from the tree toward our eyes. When we look back along the reflected rays, we see an upside-down image of the tree.

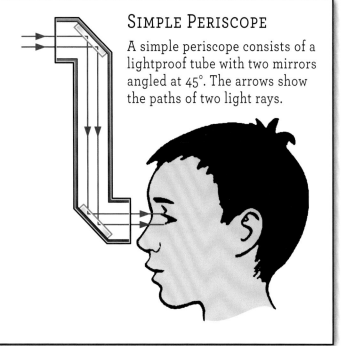

SIMPLE PERISCOPE

A simple periscope consists of a lightproof tube with two mirrors angled at 45°. The arrows show the paths of two light rays.

same-sized images of objects. The image seems to be the same distance behind the mirror as it actually is in front of the mirror. But if you look at your reflection in a mirror you will see that it is reversed left to right. Try winking your right eye, and your image winks its left eye. It is as if left and right have been interchanged. Physicists call this effect lateral inversion. But if the mirror is vertical, the image is always the right way up.

USING MIRRORS

The most common use of plane mirrors is for looking at our own reflection. Every day people use mirrors when combing their hair, when putting on makeup, or when shaving. No store that sells clothes could function without mirrors for the customers. Mirrors are also used to add light and a feeling of space to rooms. A carefully placed mirror is as good as another window for improving the light. And because it is not always obvious that we are looking at a reflection in a mirror, and not at a real object, illusionists and magicians employ mirrors for some of their on-stage trickery.

To the left you can see a diagram of a simple periscope that has two plane mirrors angled at 45°. Periscopes are used to look over obstructions, especially if you are not tall enough to see over the heads of people in front of you at a parade or sporting event. Enlarging periscopes that are used in submarines usually contain prisms instead of mirrors, as in the binoculars illustrated on page 57.

CONCAVE AND CONVEX

So far we have looked at properties of plane (flat) mirrors. Curved mirrors behave in quite a different way. There are two main types, called concave if they are curved inward like the inside of the bowl of a spoon, and convex if they are curved outward like the outside of the bowl of the spoon. The curvature gives such mirrors two further properties. Each has an axis, which is a line at right angles to the mirror that passes through its center. And the radius of curvature is the distance to the mirror from the center of a sphere of which it would form a part. The center of this sphere is also the mirror's center of curvature.

With a concave mirror, rays of light parallel to the axis are reflected to a point known as the focus. For this reason a concave mirror is also called a converging mirror. When a convex mirror reflects parallel rays, however, the reflected rays fan out to form a diverging beam. These rays all appear to come from a single point behind the mirror, which is its focus. A convex mirror is therefore also known as a diverging mirror. The concave mirror has a real focus, while the convex mirror has a virtual focus.

In both types of mirror the focal length—the distance from the mirror to the focus—is half the mirror's radius of curvature.

PLANE AND CURVED MIRRORS

Plane and curved mirrors form images in different ways. With a plane mirror (a) the image is same-sized and upright. With a concave mirror (b) and the object between the focus and the mirror, the image is magnified. With a convex mirror (c) the image is always reduced in size. (C is the center of curvature, and F is the focus.)

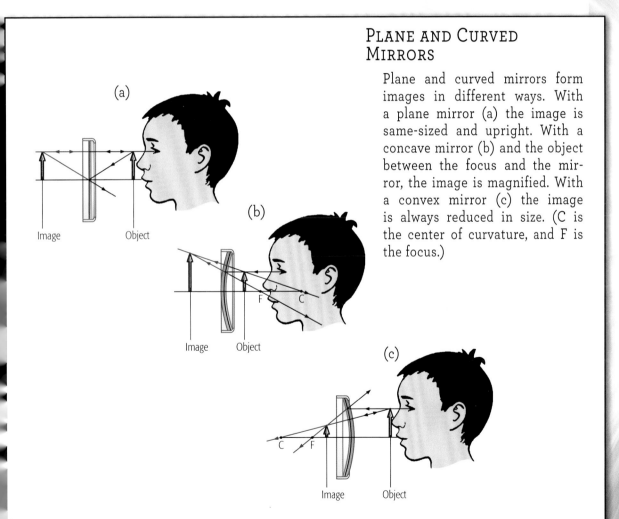

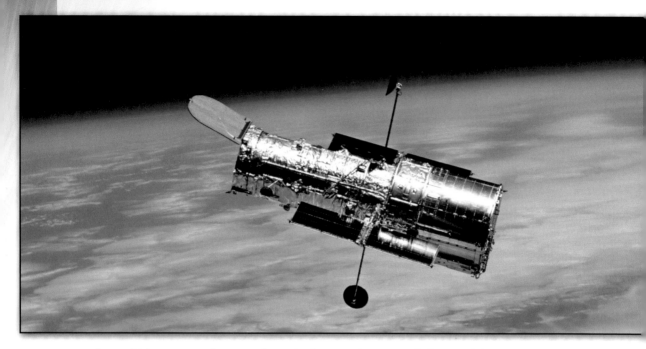

The Hubble Space Telescope, launched into orbit around the Earth by NASA in 1990, contains a 2.4 meter (7.8 ft.) concave mirror.

DIFFERENT IMAGES

The formation of images by curved mirrors is more complicated than with plane mirrors. What happens depends on whether the mirror is concave or convex, and on how far the object is from the mirror. For a concave mirror there are four different possibilities.

When the object is farther from the mirror than the center of curvature, the image is upside down, smaller than the object, and located in front of the mirror. You can see this for yourself by looking into the bowl of a polished tablespoon from just a few inches away.

When the object is moved closer to the concave mirror's center of curvature, it increases in size until, at exactly the center of curvature, the image (still inverted) is the same size as the object.

When the object is even closer to the mirror, between the center of curvature and the focus, the image is still real and inverted but it is now larger than the object. The mirror now magnifies.

Finally, when the object is between the focus and the mirror, the image becomes virtual (is formed behind the mirror), magnified, and the right way up. Such magnified images can be seen in mirrors designed to be used when

Convex driving mirrors on cars often carry a reminder that the images are closer than they appear.

shaving or putting on makeup, as is illustrated in diagram (b) on page 27.

A convex mirror always produces a reduced, upright virtual image (behind the mirror, as in diagram (c) on page 27).

It is the type used as a driving mirror for motor vehicles. Because the whole scene is reduced in size, it provides a wide angle of view. Both types of curved mirror are used in telescopes (see page 58).

CHAPTER SIX

BENDING LIGHT

When a ray of light passes from one transparent substance into another, such as from air into glass, it is bent. This bending, called refraction, happens because light moves at different speeds in different substances—and makes things appear in different places.

You may have noticed that a swimming pool looks as if it is not as deep as it really is. And fish in a lake or river appear to be nearer the surface than they really are. The reason for the illusion is that light rays traveling from underwater objects do not keep going in the same direction when they emerge through the surface and into the air.

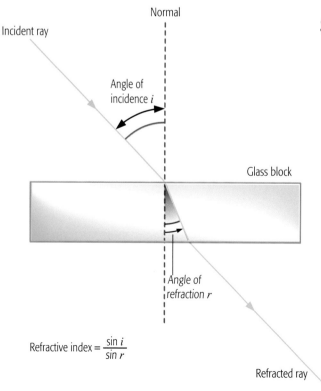

Normal

Incident ray

Angle of incidence i

Glass block

Angle of refraction r

Refractive index $= \dfrac{\sin i}{\sin r}$

Refracted ray

SNELL'S LAW

Snell's law, the chief law of refraction, states that the sine of the angle of incidence divided by the sine of the angle of refraction is a constant, known as the refractive index.

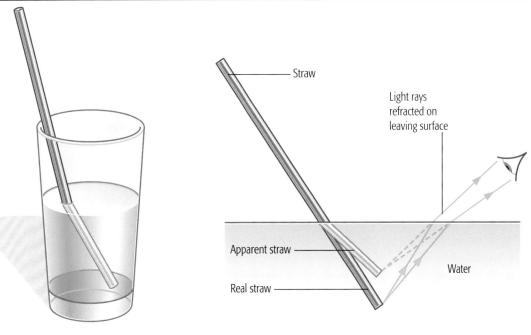

BENT STRAW

Refraction causes a straw to appear bent below the surface of water in a glass. The same effect makes a pool appear to be shallower than it really is, and for fish to look as if they are nearer the surface than they actually are.

A similar effect occurs when light rays pass from air into water. The angle between the incoming ray and the normal (a line at right angles to the surface) is called the angle of incidence. Below the water surface the angle between the light ray and the normal is called the angle of refraction. When light enters a denser medium, as when it travels from air into water or into glass, the angle of refraction is less than the angle of incidence—the ray is refracted toward the normal. When light travels from one medium into a less dense medium, as from glass into air, the angle of refraction is greater than the angle of incidence—the ray is refracted away from the normal.

As with the reflection of light, there are laws of refraction. The laws concern the angles—not the angles themselves, but a mathematical function called the sine (usually written as sin) of the angle. The chief law says that the sine of the angle of incidence ($\sin i$) divided by the sine of the angle of refraction ($\sin r$) has a constant value for any pair of media.

SLOW SUNSET

Under certain conditions, when there is a layer of denser air near the Earth's surface, the Sun appears to take longer to set than usual. It is a result of refraction, when the denser air bends light rays from the setting Sun.

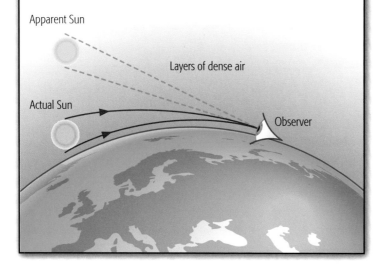

Apparent Sun

Layers of dense air

Actual Sun

Observer

REFRACTION IN ACTION

Refraction can have some strange effects. If you look at a drinking straw placed in a glass of water, the straw appears to bend below the surface. That is because light rays traveling from the straw and leaving the surface are refracted away from the normal. When we look back along the emerging rays, we see the end of the straw at a position that is apparently nearer the surface (as shown in the illustration at the top of page 31).

A similar effect can occur with the setting Sun, when the air near the surface is denser than that above it. Light rays from the Sun are refracted as they pass through this denser air. Again, looking back along the refracted rays, we see the Sun in a different position. As a result, we appear to be able to see the Sun even when it has dropped below the horizon (see the illustration above).

This ratio is known as the refractive index. For air to glass it is about 1.5, and for air to water it is about 1.33. The law is also known as Snell's law, after the Dutch physicist who first formulated it nearly 400 years ago (see page 35).

The second law of refraction states that the incident ray, the normal, and the refracted ray all lie in the same plane (just as with reflection—see pages 24–25).

MAKING OF A MIRAGE

The diagram shows how we see a mirage by looking back along the final path of curved light rays from a distant object. It also explains why the mirage is upside down. Mirages of the sky can create the appearance of lakes of water on the surface of a hot road.

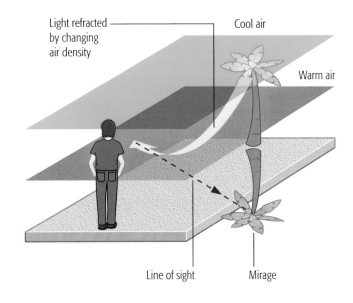

Light refracted by changing air density

Cool air

Warm air

Line of sight

Mirage

In the opposite situation, when light is traveling from dense air through less dense air, refraction also occurs, and a mirage can be the result. In this case the warm air near the ground is less dense than the colder air above it, a condition that often arises in deserts and above the surface of a highway in warm weather. Light rays from a distant object follow a curved path through the warm air. When we look back along these rays we see an image of the distant object, but the image is upside down and appears to be below the ground surface.

TOTAL INTERNAL REFLECTION

When the angle of incidence reaches a certain value, called the critical angle, the angle of refraction equals 90°. In other words, the refracted light ray travels along the boundary between the two media. This is called total internal reflection. If the angle of incidence is greater then the critical angle, there is no refraction. The incident ray is then reflected from the surface of the second medium, just as if it had struck a mirror.

USING REFRACTION

The major practical use of refraction is in lenses and in the instruments and devices that employ them. Optical prisms also make use of refraction (see page 37). A more recent application is fiber optics, in which light is "piped" along a bundle of thin fibers of glass or plastic. A succession of refractions and internal reflections occur along the length of each fiber, so that most of the light entering at one end comes out at the other end. Fiber optics are used in medical endoscopes for making examinations inside a patient's body and for long-distance telephone cables in which signals are transmitted as a series of coded flashes of light. Several thousand telephone conversations can be sent at the same time along a single optic fiber.

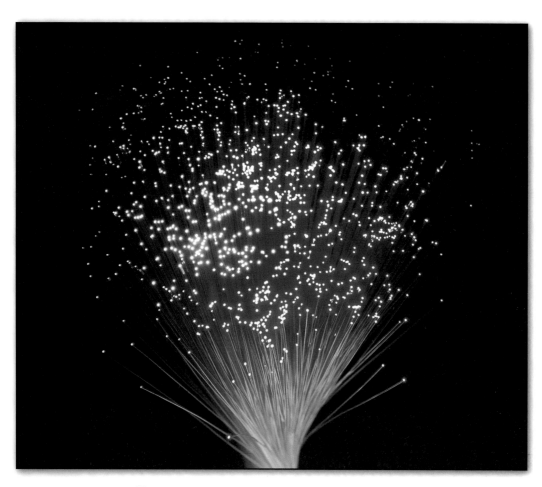

Many companies use fiber optic cables to send Internet, phone, and cable television signals into homes and businesses.

WILLEBRORD SNELL

Willebrord van Roijen Snell was born in 1580 at Leiden in the Netherlands. He trained in mathematics and physics. When his father died in 1613, he succeeded him as Professor of Mathematics at the new Leiden University. Snell specialized in land measurement and mapping and carried out many experiments on light and optics. He discovered his law of refraction in 1621 and introduced the idea of refractive index (now defined as the ratio of the sines of the angles of incidence and refraction). When Snell died in 1626, the results of his work had still not been published. It was later found that the refractive index is also equal to the ratio of the speed of light in the two media concerned.

In this mirage there is a layer of warm air over the hot desert sand. Light rays from the sky and distant hills are refracted as they pass from colder air and create upside-down images of the hills and sky.

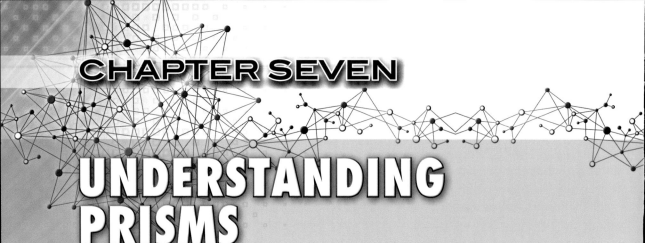

CHAPTER SEVEN

UNDERSTANDING PRISMS

Prisms are the best-known light benders. Refraction bends a light ray when it enters a prism and then bends it again when it leaves. More importantly, it bends different colors of light to a different extent. In fact, a triangular prism can split white light from the Sun into all the colors of the rainbow—a range of hues called the solar spectrum.

A triangular glass prism splits a beam of white light into a spectrum of colors that ranges from red, through orange, yellow, green, blue, and indigo, to violet. These are the colors of the rainbow.

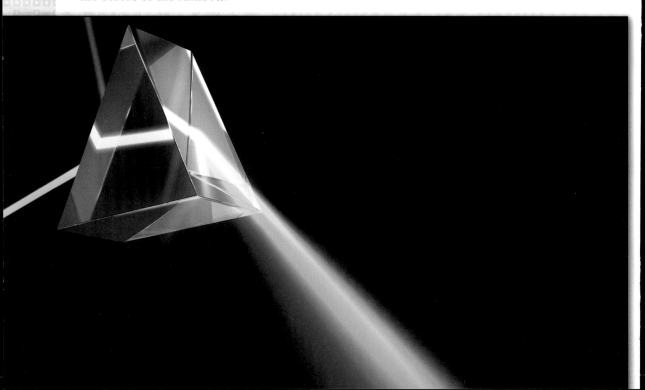

NEWTON'S EXPERIMENT

Isaac Newton used a prism to split white light into its component colors (upper diagram). He then used a filter to block all but one color—here it is red—and showed that a second prism did not split it any further.

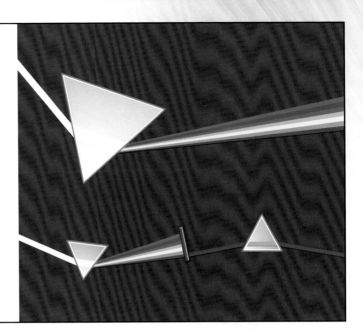

One of the most important experiments in physics took place in a darkened room in Cambridge, England, in about 1665. The physicist Isaac Newton allowed a beam of sunlight through a hole in the drapes and shone it onto a glass prism. To his surprise, parallel bands of rainbow colors appeared on the opposite wall. From this observation Newton concluded that sunlight consists of a mixture of colors that the prism had separated. When he selected just one of the colors and passed it through a second prism, there was no further change.

Modern physics can easily explain what happened in Newton's room. White light is made up of a mixture of the colors of the rainbow, ranging from red to violet with all the other colors in between. As each color enters the prism, it is refracted (bent). But red light is not bent as much as violet light. As a result, the red and violet emerge from the prism at different angles (and the in-between colors emerge at in-between angles). This has the effect of spreading white light's component colors into a spectrum. The colors are red, orange, yellow, green, blue, indigo, and violet.

This special sort of refraction by a prism is known as dispersion. And the different colors produced are called a spectrum. This accounts for the colors that can sometimes been seen when sunlight

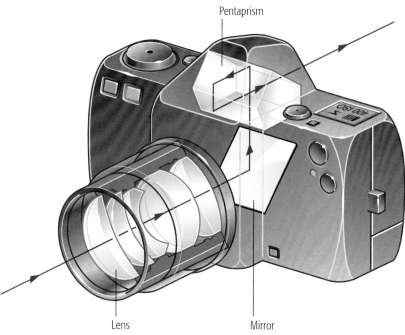

Pentaprism

Lens

Mirror

SINGLE-LENS REFLEX

There are two types of reflector in a modern single-lens reflex camera: a mirror and a five-sided prism called a pentaprism. Light entering the camera through the lens is first reflected upward by the mirror. Then two more reflections inside the pentaprism direct the light out of the viewfinder and into the photographer's eye. A pentaprism is used (and not another mirror) because the image leaving the lens is upside down, and the double reflection in the pentaprism turns the image right side up again.

shines through a crystal glass or ornamental light fitting. It also accounts for the formation of rainbows (see pages 45–46).

USING PRISMS

Prisms are used in several scientific instruments, such as spectrographs, as well as in periscopes and binoculars. But perhaps the most common use today is in the single-lens reflex camera. Everyday prisms, such as the one Newton used, are triangular in shape. But this camera uses a prism with five faces, called a pentaprism. The way it works is illustrated above.

Single-lens reflex, or SLR, cameras allow photographers to see the exact image that will be captured, unlike cameras that use viewfinders.

CHAPTER EIGHT

MIXING LIGHTS AND COLORS

White light is actually made up of a mixture of all the colors of the rainbow, as we saw on the previous pages. So why do colored objects look colored when they are illuminated with white light? And why do most colored objects change color when they are illuminated with colored light?

The illustration on the right explains why colored objects look colored. When white light illuminates a red object, for example, most of the light is absorbed by the surface of the object. Most—but not all. The red component of the white light is reflected, along with a little orange. As a result, the object appears to our eyes to be red. Similarly, a blue object reflects mostly blue light, and a yellow object reflects mostly yellow.

This explanation works only for white light. Illuminating objects with colored light can have strange effects. Try looking at the colors of cars and trucks under yellow sodium streetlights, and you will

These buildings in Buenos Aires are painted in a range of bright colors.

not be able to get the colors right. In fact, only yellow vehicles still look yellow.

PRIMARY COLORS

We have seen (page 37) that white light is a mixture of the seven colors of the rainbow. So it should come as no surprise to learn that mixing all seven colors in the right amounts produces white light. But not all seven colors are needed. You can make white light by mixing only three colors, which are known as the primary colors of light.

Light's primary colors are red, blue, and green. All three mixed together make white. But the primary colors can be mixed in pairs to make three more colors,

COLORED OBJECTS

White light is a mixture of all colors. When it shines on something colored, the object absorbs all colors except its own. This color is reflected to the eyes of the observer. A little of the neighboring colors in the spectrum are reflected as well, particularly from yellow objects.

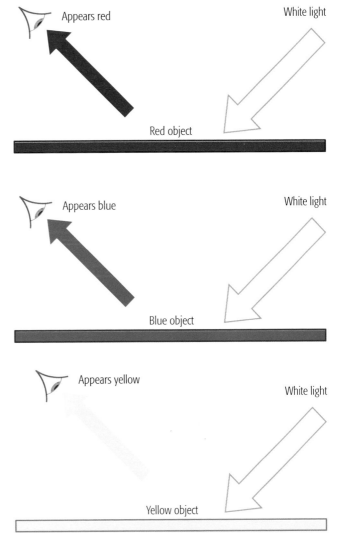

Appears red

White light

Red object

Appears blue

White light

Blue object

Appears yellow

White light

Yellow object

called secondary colors. Red and green light mix to make yellow, green and blue mix to make a brighter blue called cyan, and blue and red mix to make a pinkish red called magenta.

A mixture of the three secondary colors again produces white light. In fact, careful mixing of the three primary or secondary colors of light will produce any color you can think of. If you look at a television picture up real close, you will see that it is made up of lots of tiny colored dots. Look even closer, and you will see that there are only three kinds of colored dots: red, green, and blue—the primary colors. In this way the correct mixture of dots produces the complete range of colors on the television screen.

The colors of a color transparency photograph are produced in much the same way. Because the colors are added to make new colors, this type of color mixing is called the additive process. It is commonly used in theaters and light shows where colored spotlights are mixed to produce areas of different

COLORED LIGHTS

The primary colors of light—red, blue, and green—mix by the additive process to produce white light. The same colors mix in pairs to form the secondary colors of light—yellow, cyan, and magneta.

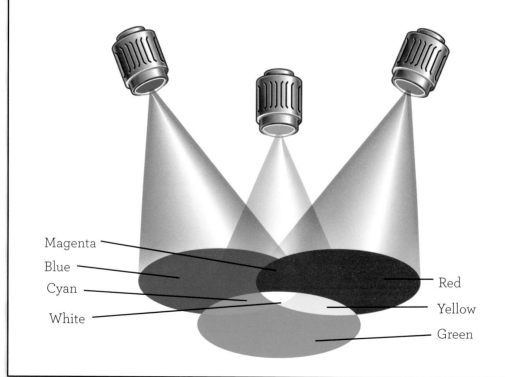

Magenta

Blue

Cyan

White

Red

Yellow

Green

colors. The colored lights are usually produced by placing a transparent colored filter in front of a white light. A red filter, for example, absorbs all colors except red, which passes through to make a red light. A green filter absorbs every color except green. It is particularly good at absorbing red; so if you put a red filter and a green filter in front of a white light, no light at all gets through. You can try this for yourself with the thin colored plastic used to wrap candy.

MIXING PAINTS

So far we have been considering what happens when you mix colored lights.

More familiar to most people is the effect of mixing paints, inks, and other pigments. You have probably tried it with paints from a paintbox. If you have, you will know that mixing all the colors together produces a muddy black color. This should give you a clue as to what happens when mixing paints.

As with colored lights, colored paints have three primary colors. They are yellow, cyan, and magenta (exactly the same as the secondary colors of light). A mixture of all three primary colors produces black. Mixing the primary colors in pairs produces the secondary colors of paint. Yellow and magneta mix to make red, magneta and cyan mix to make blue, and

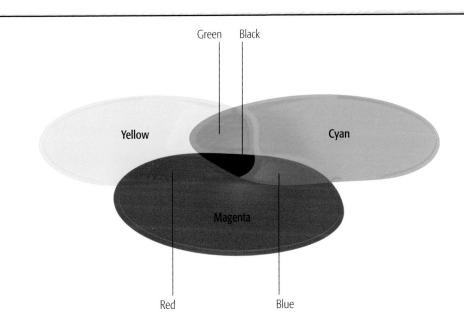

COLORED PAINTS

The primary colors of paint—yellow, cyan, and magenta—mix by the subtractive process to produce black. The same colors mix in pairs to form the secondary colors of paint—red, blue, and green.

cyan and yellow mix to produce green. Notice that the secondary colors of paint are the same as the primary colors of light.

When yellow and magenta paints are mixed, this has the effect of removing blue and green from black, which leaves red. Similarly, mixing magenta and cyan removes red and green to leave blue, and mixing cyan and yellow removes red and blue to leave green. Artists learn how to make other colors by mixing. In fact, some artists use very few individual colors and make all the others they need by combining them. Because mixing colored paints effectively removes colors from black, it is called the subtractive process.

The most common application of the subtractive process is in color printing. If you have a powerful magnifying glass, look at one of the colored illustrations in this book. You will see that it is made up of tiny dots of color. There are only three colors present: yellow, cyan, and magenta—the three primary colors of paint. By varying the sizes and numbers of the various colored dots, the printing process has produced all possible colors. Indeed, in the photograph below, we can quite truthfully say that the printing process has reproduced all the colors of the rainbow!

A bright rainbow arches down to the trees below. Around this bow, at a slightly greater height, a faint secondary rainbow can just be seen. Its colors are in the opposite order from those in the primary rainbow.

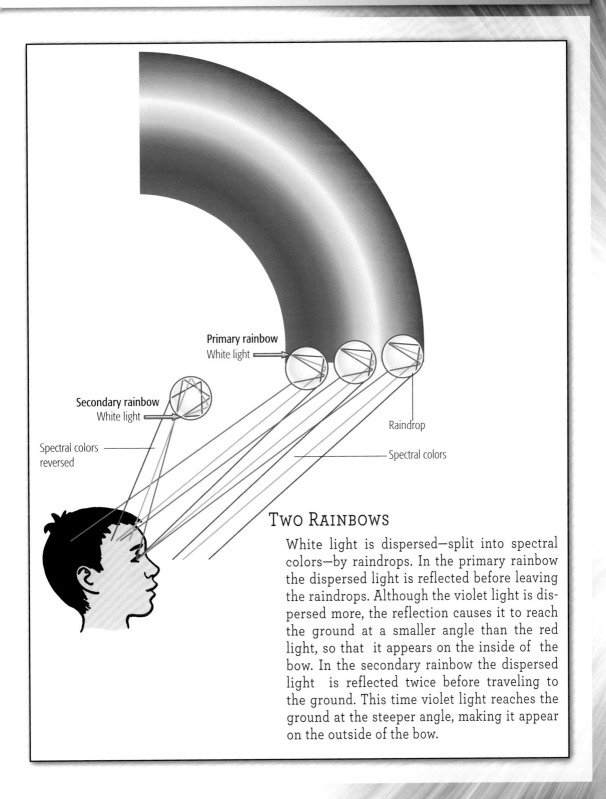

Primary rainbow
White light

Secondary rainbow
White light

Spectral colors
reversed

Raindrop

Spectral colors

Two Rainbows

White light is dispersed—split into spectral colors—by raindrops. In the primary rainbow the dispersed light is reflected before leaving the raindrops. Although the violet light is dispersed more, the reflection causes it to reach the ground at a smaller angle than the red light, so that it appears on the inside of the bow. In the secondary rainbow the dispersed light is reflected twice before traveling to the ground. This time violet light reaches the ground at the steeper angle, making it appear on the outside of the bow.

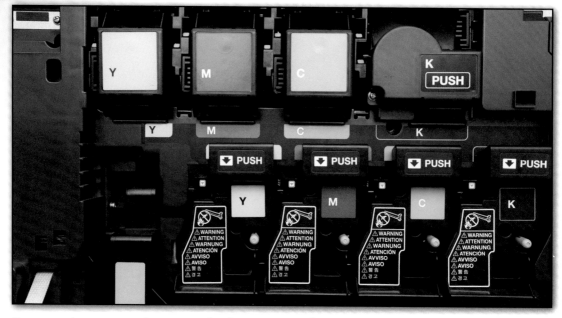

Laser copiers can produce any color by using just four colors of toner, seen here.

HOW DO RAINBOWS FORM?

The clue to how a rainbow is formed is in the first part of its name—rain. Rainbows generally appear just before or after a sudden rainstorm on a sunny day. These two things are essential: raindrops in the air and sunshine. The raindrops disperse the white light of the Sun—that is, they split it into a spectrum of colors as a prism does (see pages 36–37). If you look carefully you can sometimes see a second faint rainbow around the outside of the main bow. But the order of the colors is reversed in the secondary rainbow.

The rainbow is an arc of a circle and is always in the part of the sky opposite the Sun. As we look at a rainbow, white light coming from behind us enters near the top of a raindrop, is dispersed and reflected inside the drop, and is then refracted downward as it leaves the drop. Different colors are refracted through different angles, so they appear to be separated in the rainbow. This is called the primary rainbow.

In the secondary rainbow light enters near the bottom of a drop, is dispersed, and is reflected twice before being angled toward the ground. The angle is steeper, which is why a secondary rainbow appears higher in the sky than the primary bow.

The double reflection inside the raindrops also has the effect of changing the order of the spectral colors. As a result, the secondary rainbow has colors in reverse order from those in a primary rainbow, with violet on the outside of the bow.

CHAPTER NINE

LIGHT THROUGH A LENS

We saw earlier how a ray of light is refracted, or bent, when it enters a rectangular block of glass (see page 30). A curved block of glass has the same effect; but because the angles of incidence change around the curve, a lens can bend whole bundles of light rays through different angles. Lenses can be either concave or convex.

There are two main kinds of lens, named either after their shape or after the effect they have on rays of light that pass through them. A lens whose surfaces bulge outward is called a convex lens (like a convex mirror). This is the type of lens that is used as a magnifying glass. But because parallel light rays that pass through a convex lens converge (come together) to a focus on the other side of the lens, a convex lens is also commonly referred to as a converging lens.

A lens whose surfaces are curved inward is called a concave lens (like a concave mirror). It

Camera lenses come in many sizes and colors.

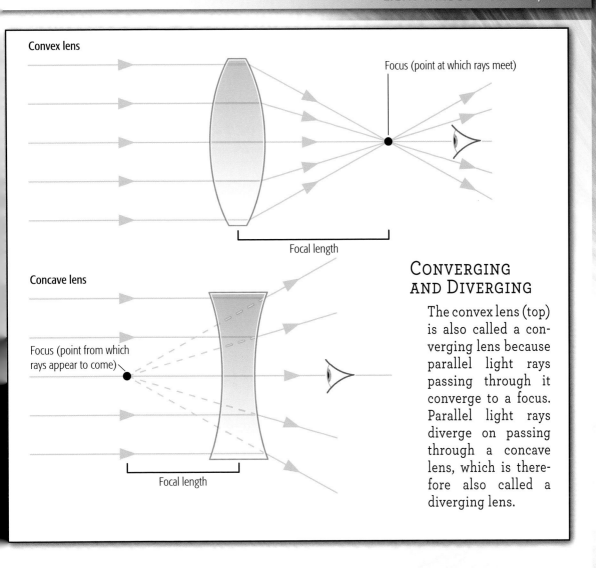

Convex lens

Focus (point at which rays meet)

Focal length

Concave lens

Focus (point from which rays appear to come)

Focal length

CONVERGING AND DIVERGING

The convex lens (top) is also called a converging lens because parallel light rays passing through it converge to a focus. Parallel light rays diverge on passing through a concave lens, which is therefore also called a diverging lens.

is the type of lens used in eyeglasses for shortsighted people. Parallel light rays passing through a concave lens diverge (spread out), and the focus is on the same side as the incident light. For this reason a concave lens is also referred to as a diverging lens.

MAGNIFY OR REDUCE

We have already noted that a convex lens can be used as a magnifying glass. The diagram on page 50 shows how it works. Parallel light rays from an object converge toward a focus, and when we look

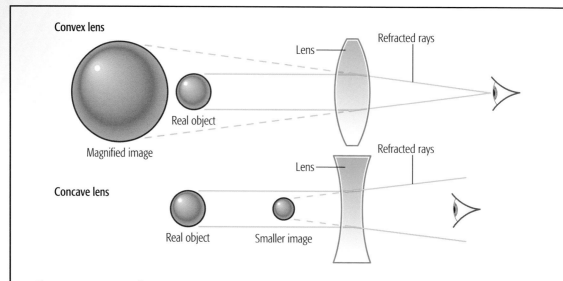

Convex lens

Magnified image

Real object

Lens

Refracted rays

Concave lens

Real object

Smaller image

Lens

Refracted rays

LARGER AND SMALLER

Convex and concave lenses have opposite effects on the size of images they produce. A convex lens magnifies, and the greater the curvature of the lens, the more it magnifies. The earliest microscopes, made more than 300 years ago, had a single, almost spherical convex lens. The image produced by a concave lens is smaller than the object.

back along these rays, we see a magnified image of the object. With a concave lens the light rays diverge toward the observer's eye. Looking back along these rays reveals a diminished image of the object. Artists and designers sometimes use a diverging lens, which they call a reducing glass, to check how a large image will appear when it is reduced in size.

LENS ABERRATIONS

If you look at an object through a simple convex lens, you can often see colored fringes around the edge of the image. This effect is called chromatic aberration (any fault in a lens is known as an aberration). It happens because the edges of the lens refracts blue light more than red

CHROMATIC ABERRATION AND ITS CURE

Chromatic aberration, which produces colored fringes around the edges of images, arises with a single lens because blue and red light are focused at different points. Adding a second concave lens made from a different kind of glass can cure it.

Chromatic aberration

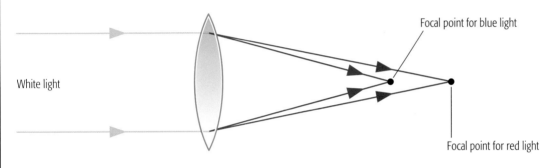

White light

Focal point for blue light

Focal point for red light

Achromatic lens

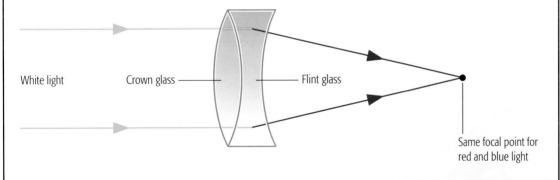

White light   Crown glass ——   —— Flint glass

Same focal point for red and blue light

ERNST ABBE

Ernst Abbe, who was born in 1840, was a German physicist and professor of physics at the University of Jena in eastern Germany. The university obtained its optical instruments from a local supplier named Carl Zeiss. Abbe is best known for his collaboration with Zeiss in the production of better-quality lenses, particularly for microscopes. Abbe's knowledge of optics and mathematics combined with Zeiss's practical skills—and the contribution of a glassmaker named Otto Schott—led to the production of new types of lenses with fewer aberrations. Abbe also developed a condenser lens system for concentrating the light on a specimen placed under a microscope. The tradition established by these men continues, and Jena is still well known for its manufacture of high-quality cameras and other optical instruments.

light, so that the two colors are focused at different points. It can be corrected by adding a concave lens made from a different kind of glass, which makes the blue rays diverge and come to the same focus as the red rays. The resulting combination is called an achromatic lens (or achromat).

In another type of aberration the image produced by a lens is fuzzy because light rays passing through the edge of the lens come to a different focus than do light rays that pass through the center of the lens. This defect, called spherical aberration, is cured by placing a plate with a central hole, called a stop or aperture, in front of the lens, as in a camera. Light can only pass through the center of the lens, so the result is an in-focus, sharp image.

The Friedrich Schiller University Jena is one of the oldest universities in Germany.

PREVENTING FUZZY IMAGES

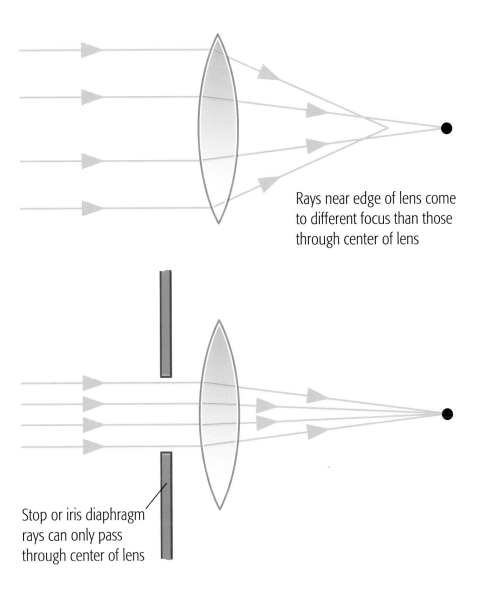

Rays near edge of lens come to different focus than those through center of lens

Stop or iris diaphragm rays can only pass through center of lens

Light passing through the outer edges of a simple lens is brought to a different focus than light that passes through the center. As a result, the image is fuzzy and out of focus. A stop or diaphragm allows only the central rays to pass, resulting in a sharp image.

Light has been defined as the only type of radiation that we can see. But we could not see anything at all if we did not have eyes. And the human eye is a natural application of a lens. Understanding how lenses work therefore gives us an understanding of the human eye and of some of the defects of human vision and how to correct them.

The main parts of the human eye are shown in the illustration on the right. The lens and its supporting structures divide the eyeball into two unequal chambers. The front chamber contains a watery liquid called aqueous humor. The jellylike vitreous humor fills the larger chamber. The eyeball itself is transparent at the front, at the cornea, so that light can enter. A thin layer of tears keeps the cornea moist.

The lens is supported by ciliary muscles, which can also pull on the lens to change its shape to focus on objects. The lens is stretched and made thinner when we look at distant objects, and allowed to get thicker (by relaxing the ciliary muscles) when we look at nearby objects. The colored iris in front of the lens has a central hole called the pupil. The iris can change size to vary the size of the pupil. The pupil is large in dim light, so that it can admit as much light as possible, but in bright light the iris closes down to make the pupil much smaller.

UPSIDE-DOWN IMAGES

The light-sensitive retina lines the inside of the eyeball, and the lens focuses an upside-down image of objects onto the retina. There the light triggers nerve

The colored part of the eye is the iris, which surrounds the black pupil. Light from everything we see passes through the pupil and into the eyeball.

impulses, which pass along the optic nerve to the brain. The brain then combines the impulses from both eyes, converts them into "pictures" that we can see, and turns them the right way up.

COMMON DEFECTS

In two of the most common defects of eyesight, light rays are not focused correctly on the retina. In a longsighted person the eyeball is too short front-to-back. As a result the eye's lens tries to focus light rays at a point behind the retina. This condition is corrected with eyeglasses made from convex lenses or by convex contact lenses. They make the rays converge in focus onto the retina.

In a shortsighted person the eyeball is too long front-to-back. The eye's lens brings light rays to a focus that lies in front of the retina. To improve their vision, shortsighted people wear eyeglasses made from concave lenses or concave contact lenses. They make the rays diverge slightly, so that they come to the right focus on the retina.

Another common eye defect, called astigmatism, arises when the transparent cornea at the front of the eyeball is not perfectly spherical. When looking at a cross like a plus sign (+) with an astigmatic eye, either the upright part of the cross is in focus and the horizontal part is not, or vice versa. The condition is corrected with eyeglasses or contact lenses that have a similar fault, but at right angles to that of the eye. Such lenses are called anastigmatic.

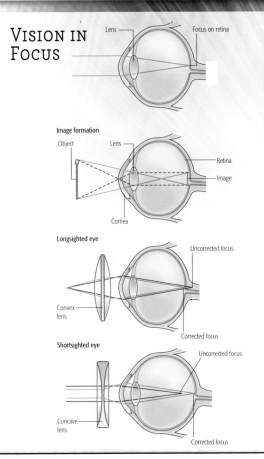

VISION IN FOCUS

Lens — Focus on retina

Image formation
Object — Lens — Retina — Image — Cornea

Longsighted eye — Convex lens — Uncorrected focus — Corrected focus

Shortsighted eye — Concave lens — Uncorrected focus — Corrected focus

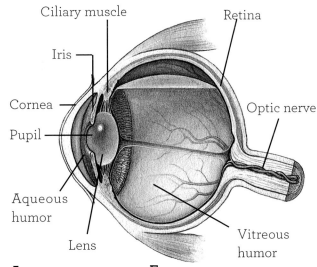

Ciliary muscle — Retina
Iris — Cornea — Optic nerve
Pupil — Aqueous humor — Lens — Vitreous humor

ANATOMY OF THE EYE

Important parts of the eye include the lens and the cornea. Both help in focusing, although only the lens is adjustable—it does most of the work.

CHAPTER ELEVEN
MAGNIFYING WITH INSTRUMENTS

The main components of optical devices are mirrors, lenses, and prisms. The workings of all of them have been dealt with earlier in this book. Now we look at how they are put to practical use in various kinds of optical instruments.

Nowadays nearly everyone owns at least one camera, which is therefore the most common optical device. In many ways a camera works like the human eye (described on the previous pages). It has a lens, a variable aperture, and a light-sensitive surface. The lens focuses the image, the aperture controls the amount of light entering the camera, and the film records the image focused onto it by the

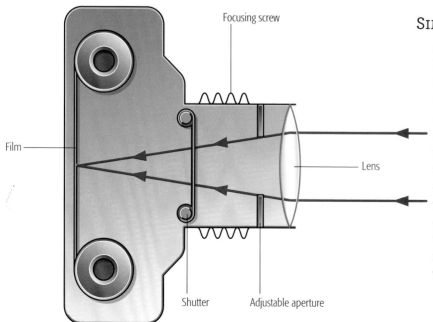

Focusing screw

Film

Lens

Shutter   Adjustable aperture

SIMPLE CAMERA

A camera is basically a lightproof box that holds light-sensitive film. A lens focuses an image of the object to be photographed onto the film. The lens can be screwed in or out slightly to focus the image. An adjustable aperture, called an iris diaphragm, can be altered in size to control the amount of light entering the camera. The amount of light that falls on the film is also determined by the length of time for which the shutter is open.

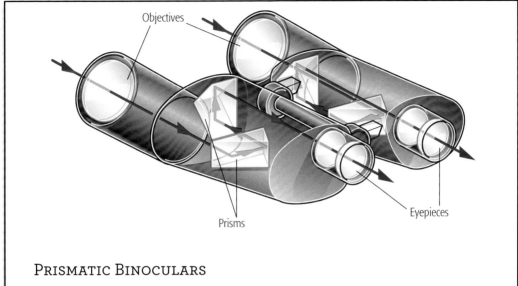

Objectives

Prisms

Eyepieces

PRISMATIC BINOCULARS

A pair of prisms "fold" the optical path in each side of the binoculars, thereby shortening the instrument and turning the image the right way up.

lens. The image is actually upside down, but of course this does not matter. In addition a camera has a shutter that controls the amount of time (in fractions of a second) for which light is allowed into the camera and onto the film.

In order to focus the object being photographed—depending on how far away it is—the lens can be moved farther from or nearer to the film. This is usually achieved by rotating the lens mount, which has a fine screw thread. In very old cameras, as well as some specialized modern ones, the lens is mounted on a bellows arrangement and racks backward or forward to focus the camera. In this respect the camera is different from the human eye, in which the lens changes shape in order to focus. But there are

animals that focus their eyes just like a camera by moving the lens in and out—an octopus, for example, can do this.

A device called a viewfinder allows the photographer to aim the camera accurately. The viewfinder of a simple camera is a pair of small lenses. In a single-lens reflex camera a pentaprism forms the viewfinder (see page 38). Some cameras have interchangeable lenses—alternative lenses for different tasks. They range from wide-angle lenses with short focal lengths to long-focus telephoto lenses for taking close-ups of distant objects.

Digital cameras have dispensed with film altogether and use computer technology to record images, but they still rely on traditional lens systems to form the image.

USING TELESCOPES

A telephoto lens for use with a camera is basically a type of telescope. The more usual kind of telescope, used by naturalists to study wildlife, by amateur astronomers, and by shooters to see where their shots have hit the target, consists of a long tube with a lens at each end. The front lens is the objective lens, and the rear one is the eyepiece. With two convex lenses the image is upside down, although this does not usually matter in astronomy (that is why early drawings and photographs of the Moon that were made using a telescope have the Moon's north pole at the bottom). A third convex lens may be positioned inside the telescope tube to turn the image the right way up.

If the eyepiece is a concave lens, the image is the right way up. This type is known as a Galilean telescope, after the Italian scientist Galileo Galilei, who used this same design in his pioneering astronomical studies nearly 400 years ago. A pair of Galilean telescopes side by side form opera glasses, sometimes used by people seated toward the back of a theater to get a better view of the performance on stage.

Paired telescopes are also employed in binoculars. Powerful telescopes are long and difficult to hold without a stand or a mounting. And, as we have seen, they produce an inverted image. All of these difficulties are overcome in prismatic

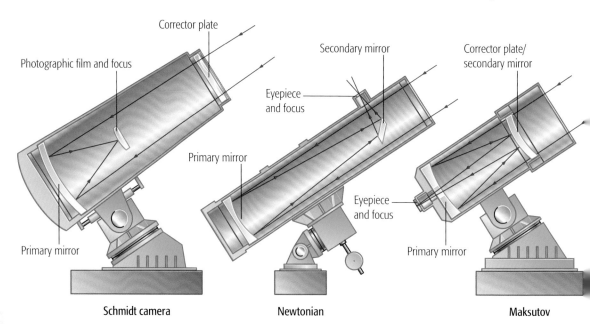

Corrector plate

Photographic film and focus

Secondary mirror

Corrector plate/
secondary mirror

Eyepiece
and focus

Primary mirror

Eyepiece
and focus

Primary mirror

Primary mirror

Primary mirror

Schmidt camera

Newtonian

Maksutov

REFLECTING TELESCOPES

The Schmidt camera is used mainly for photographing large areas of the night sky. Its primary mirror is an easy-to-make spherical mirror. The Newtonian reflector avoids spherical aberration by having a primary mirror with a cross section in the form of a parabola. The Maksutov telescope uses a corrector plate to overcome spherical aberration.

COMPOUND MICROSCOPE

This laboratory micro-scope has a three-lens turret with objective lenses of different strengths. The stage is racked up or down to focus the instrument, using a coarse control for the main movement and the fine control for final adjustment. The con-denser concentrates light onto the specimen. The yellow "tube" shows the path of light through the instrument.

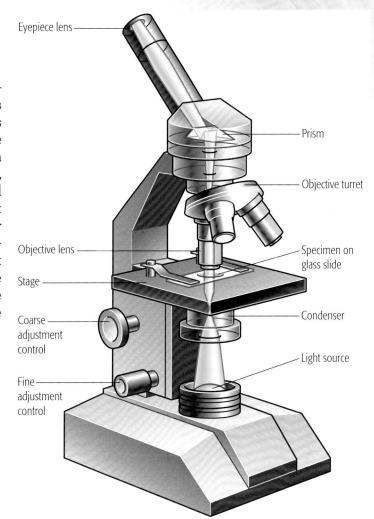

Eyepiece lens

Prism

Objective turret

Objective lens

Specimen on glass slide

Stage

Coarse adjustment control

Condenser

Fine adjustment control

Light source

binoculars, in which each telescope has a pair of prisms that "fold" the optical path back and forth to shorten it. They are also arranged at right angles to each other, so that the final image is the right way up.

REFLECTORS

Modern astronomers need really power-ful telescopes. These types have curved mirrors instead of lenses. Large mirrors are easier to make and are much lighter in weight than are big lenses. There are various designs of mirror telescope, which are called reflecting telescopes or reflectors (telescopes with lenses are known as refracting telescopes or refractors). Isaac Newton made the first reflector. It had a single curved mirror at the bottom of a tube, with a small plane mirror angled near the other end. Light rays are reflected by the plane mirror to

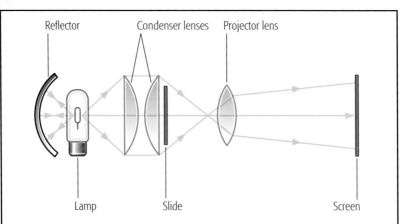

SLIDE PROJECTOR

The optical system of a slide projector includes a curved mirror that acts as a reflector to direct light from a lamp onto the condenser. The condenser evens out the light, which then passes through the slide. Finally, a lens projects an enlarged image of the slide onto a distant screen.

the eyepiece at the side of the telescope. This design is still used for telescopes for amateur astronomers. Another popular type of amateur telescope is called the Schmidt–Cassegrain and is something like a small Schmidt camera, but with an eyepiece behind a hole in the main mirror, as in the Maksutov (see the illustration).

The latest types of astronomical telescope used by professional astronomers have mirrors of up to 10 meters (33 ft) across. Computer-controlled arms below the mirror adjust its shape to keep its curvature exactly right. Some very large mirrors are composed of many hexagonal panels, resembling a honeycomb. A computer controls the positions of the panels. Astronomical telescopes are mounted in large domed buildings, which can be rotated to aim the telescope at any part of the sky. The observatories are often located on high mountains, where the air is clearer, resulting in better images.

MAGNIFYING IMAGES

Microscopes produce enlarged images of very small objects. As mentioned on page 50, the very first microscopes had a single, small convex lens. This type, called the simple microscope, was first made by a Dutch cloth-seller named Anton van Leeuwenhoek in about 1670. His best instruments magnified more than 260 times, and with them he was able to examine bacteria and blood cells.

To obtain higher magnifications, a compound microscope is used. It has a small but powerful objective lens. The image formed by the objective (a convex lens) is further enlarged by the eyepiece lens, also convex. In use the microscope is adjusted so that the object being examined is just beyond the focal length of the objective lens. This produces an enlarged inverted image inside the microscope tube. The image is just inside the focal length of the eyepiece lens, which acts like a magnifying glass to produce a greatly enlarged final image. The image remains inverted, but this seldom matters in most applications.

Most laboratory microscopes have a turret with two or three objectives of different magnifying powers. The operator rotates the turret to bring the required lens into position. A glass slide on which is placed the specimen to be examined is mounted on a stage and illuminated from below by a bulb or by light reflected from a curved mirror. A pair of lenses called a condenser concentrate the light on the specimen. For some studies, such as the examination of geological rock specimens, a binocular microscope is often used. This is essentially a compound microscope equipped with two eyepieces.

PROJECTORS

We saw earlier how a camera works. One type of photograph that can be produced

Microscopes have been used for hundreds of years. Newer digital microscopes can create images on computer screens and do not use eyepieces.

is a color transparency, commonly known as a slide. A slide can be viewed by holding it up to the light, but of course the image is very small and difficult to examine in detail. A better way of viewing it is to project an enlarged image of the slide onto a screen. This is the function of a slide projector.

In a slide projector, condenser lenses concentrate light from an electric lamp onto the slide and illuminate it evenly. Some condensers also incorporate a heat filter to avoid damaging the slide. The light passes through the slide, and the projector lens forms the image on the screen. The lens can be moved in or out slightly in order to focus the image. The image is actually upside down, which is why slides have to be inserted upside down into the projector (resulting in an image that is the right way up!).

A movie projector is optically much the same. It has in addition a mechanism to move the film through the projector and a shutter that opens and closes rapidly (usually 24 times every second). Each individual picture, or frame, of the film is stationary when the shutter is open. Then, when the shutter closes, the film moves on to the next frame. So when we go to the movies, we are actually seeing 24 still pictures each second. But our brain ignores the brief black screens between consecutive images, and we "see" continuous movement. A movie camera has a similar shutter arrangement, but in every other respect it is optically like the still camera described earlier.

This 3D image of bacteria has been magnified many times. The actual bacteria cells are only a few micrometers long.

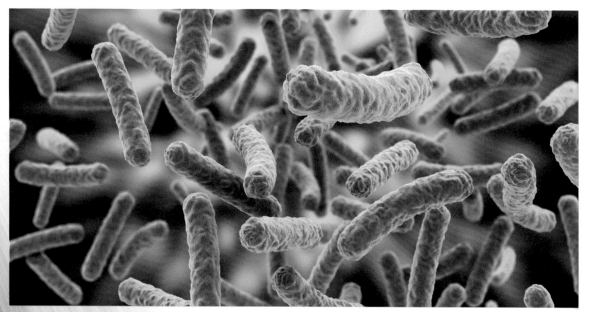

A battery of news photographers aim their cameras at a celebrity. They are using powerful telephoto lenses, and most have a monopod to help keep the camera steady.

CHAPTER TWELVE

WAVES AND INTERFERENCE

Many phenomena in which light plays a part are best explained by considering it as a wave motion. One of these is a phenomenon called interference, in which two light waves interact when they come together. Interference is behind the metallic sheen of a *butterfly's wings and the colors of an oil slick on a puddle.*

A light wave can be considered as a series of peaks and troughs traveling through the air (or through space—light will travel through a vacuum). The distance between two neigboring peaks, or troughs, is the wavelength of the light. Light wavelengths are extremely small: around 600 nanometers (6 ten-millionths of a meter, or 6 × 10–7 m).

When light waves from two different sources come together, various things can happen. If they have the same wavelength, the peaks of one wave may coincide with the

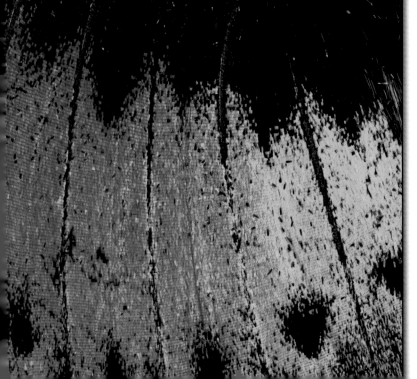

On these magnified butterfly wings, you can see tiny ridges from which blue light is reflected out of step, giving the wings a brilliant blue color.

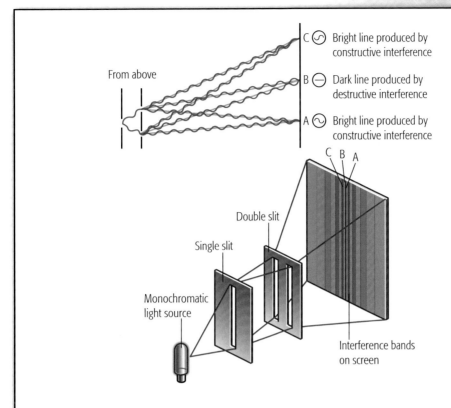

From above

C ⊘ Bright line produced by constructive interference

B ⊖ Dark line produced by destructive interference

A ⊙ Bright line produced by constructive interference

C B A

Double slit

Single slit

Monochromatic light source

Interference bands on screen

INTERFERENCE PATTERNS

Light from a monochromatic light source passes first through one and then through two slits. The two beams from the slits interfere when they reach a screen some distance away to produce a series of alternating bright and dark bands. The central band A is the brightest. Farther away from A the contrast between neighboring bands gets less.

peaks of the other wave. This produces a combined wave with even higher peaks, making a brighter light, in the phenomenon called constructive interference. If the peaks of one wave coincide with the troughs of the other, the waves tend to cancel each other out, producing a dimmer light, in destructive interference.

Interference can be demonstrated with the setup illustrated above. It requires a monochromatic light source. Monochromatic light is light of a single pure color and a single wavelength. Here monochromatic light passes through one slit and then through two slits, making it effectively two sources. But because the two beams are from the same bulb, they have exactly the same wavelength.

The light from the two slits travels to a screen. In some places two waves arrive

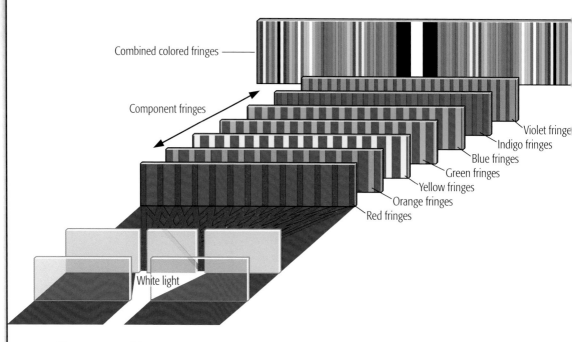

Combined colored fringes

Component fringes

Violet fringe
Indigo fringes
Blue fringes
Green fringes
Yellow fringes
Orange fringes
Red fringes

White light

COLORED FRINGES

When white light passes through a pair of slits it produces multicolored fringes. The colors are a combination of seven different sets of fringes, one for each color in the rainbow—the spectral colors that make up white light.

at the screen in step, constructive interference takes place, and a bright band of light appears on the screen. When two waves arrive at the screen out of step, destructive interference occurs, and there is a dark band on the screen. The bands get gradually fainter away from the center (because the light has to travel farther to each band). Interference bands such as these are also called fringes.

CREATING FRINGES

If two light waves of different wavelengths interfere, a complex waveform results, with some larger peaks and some smaller ones. This type of interference is known as beats. It got its name from a very similar phenomenon in sound (sound waves also undergo interference). When two notes (sounds) that are of different wavelengths interfere, you can hear a regular droning sound that varies in volume—called beats.

We learned earlier that white light, such as sunlight, is made up of a mixture of wavelengths. If we were to do an experiment similar to that just described using white light, we would create a pattern of colored fringes. Each component wavelength of the white light produces its own set of fringes, and they combine to make the overall pattern (see the illustration on the opposite page).

It is this type of interference that is responsible for several common phenomena. In the natural world a peacock's feathers and the wings of some butterflies have an iridescent sheen. The waves of light reflected from tiny ridges on the peacock's feathers or from the scales that cover a butterfly's wings get out of step, and interference occurs. When a very thin film of oil floats on water, light is reflected from the top of the oil film as well as from the surface of the water below the film. They behave as if they were two sources of light; and when their waves interfere, shimmering rainbow colors can be seen on the oil. A similar effect produces spectral colors on soap bubbles, but here light is reflected from each side of the thin film of soap that forms the bubble.

CIRCULAR INTERFERENCE

This is the name of yet another optical effect discovered by Isaac Newton. Newton's rings are circular interference fringes. The rings can be produced experimentally by setting a plano-convex lens (that is, a convex lens with one flat surface) with its curved side face-down on a mirror. When the arrangement is illuminated with monochromatic light, some of the light is reflected from the curved surface of the lens, and some passes through the lens to be reflected off the mirror.

LASER LIGHT

Atoms in the ruby crystal emit light when they absorb energy from the flash tube. This light then stimulates more atoms to give off light, which bounces between the mirrors at the ends of the crystal. Coherent red laser light leaves through a hole in one mirror.

Ruby crystal

Mirror with central hole

Coherent light

Mirror

Laser beam

Flash tube

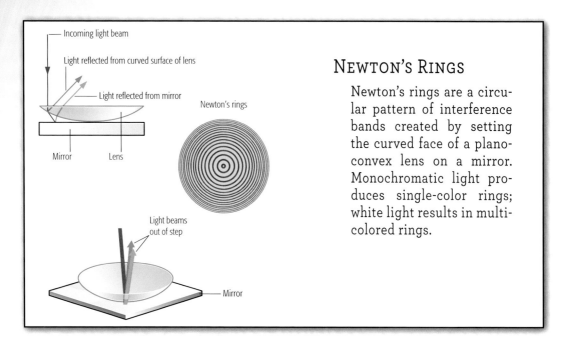

Incoming light beam

Light reflected from curved surface of lens

Light reflected from mirror

Newton's rings

Mirror   Lens

Light beams out of step

Mirror

NEWTON'S RINGS

Newton's rings are a circular pattern of interference bands created by setting the curved face of a planoconvex lens on a mirror. Monochromatic light produces single-color rings; white light results in multicolored rings.

Because the two light paths are slightly different in length, they get out of step, and interference occurs. The interference pattern takes the form of alternate light and dark concentric rings. If the experiment is repeated with white light, colored rings can be seen. Troublesome colored Newton's rings can form with photographic slides in glass mounts because the glass and the transparency are held fractionally apart. The rings can even be projected onto a screen along with the image on the slide.

COHERENT WAVES

So far we have been considering what can happen when light waves get out of step. Waves that are perfectly in step are termed coherent. For example, radio waves from a transmitter's antenna are coherent. A laser produces coherent light waves, which are also monochromatic.

"Laser" is an abbreviation of the jawbreaking term "light amplification by stimulated emission of radiation." The laser material can be a solid, such as a ruby crystal, or a gas, such as a mixture of helium and neon. Light energy from a flash tube energizes atoms of the laser material. Some of these atoms give off light, which stimulates more atoms to emit light in the same direction. Mirrors at each end of the laser bounce the light backward and forward, so that it gets stronger and stronger. The laser beam emerges from a central hole in one of the mirrors. Lasers have various applications in medicine, industry, and communications. They are also used to scan compact discs in CD players and in computers.

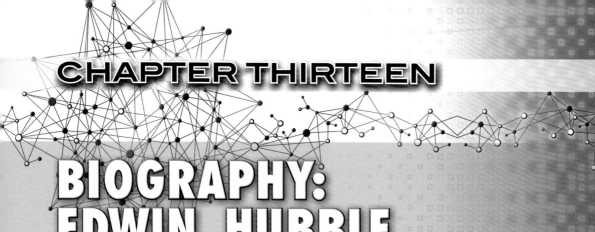

CHAPTER THIRTEEN

BIOGRAPHY: EDWIN HUBBLE

Edwin Hubble was an American astronomer who extended our view of the universe farther than anyone since the Italian astronomer Galileo Galilei (1564-1642). Hubble demonstrated that there are billions of star systems outside our own galaxy. He also discovered that these distant galaxies are moving away from ours and the farther away from us they are, the faster they are traveling.

Edwin Hubble was born in Marshfield, Missouri, the son of a lawyer. After graduating from the University of Chicago in 1910 he won a Rhodes scholarship to Oxford University, in England, where he studied law. By his own report, he was a talented athlete: a rower, runner, and boxer. One of his boxing opponents was French man named Georges Carpentier (1894-1975). Carpentier went on to achieve worldwide fame in 1921 when he was beaten by American Jack Dempsey (1895-1983) in the most highly publicized world heavyweight championship fight yet staged.

Back in America, Hubble worked for a short time for a law practice in

Some of Edwin Hubble's observations are considered proof of the big bang theory.

Mount Wilson Observatory's 60-inch Hale telescope is the largest telescope in the world used mainly by the general public.

Kentucky. But his heart was not in the law, and in 1914 he went back to college, this time to study astronomy at the Yerkes Observatory at Williams Bay, Wisconsin, part of the University of Chicago (he is supposed to have said he would rather be a second-rate astronomer than a first-rate lawyer). He obtained a Ph.D. in astronomy in 1917, and after a short spell serving with the U.S. Army in France during World War I (1914–18), joined the staff of the Mount Wilson Observatory, in Pasadena, California, in 1919. There he remained for the rest of his career.

DEBATING THE UNIVERSE

Hubble entered serious astronomy just as a major argument was raging in the science. The debate was about the size and structure of the universe.

American astronomer Harlow Shapley (1885–1972), working at the Mount Wilson Observatory, took the view that the Milky Way, our own galaxy, more or less made up the whole of the universe. He observed that the Milky Way is disk-shaped and measures about 300,000 light-years across (a light-year is equivalent to the distance that light travels in a vacuum in one year—about 5.8 trillion miles). To map the structure of the universe, Shapley used the discovery of American astronomer Henrietta Leavitt (1868–1921) concerning a type of star called a Cepheid variable, which provided the key to measuring very large distances in space.

Shapley calculated the relative distances of star clusters containing Cepheid variables from Earth and from each other. His calculations were overgenerous—he was unaware that interstellar matter (thin dispersals of gases and dust between stars) absorbs some of the light from stars and so affects determinations of their brightness, or magnitude. The diameter of the galaxy was later revised to 100,000 light-years.

In 1920, a debate was held at the National Academy of Sciences between Shapley and astronomer Heber Curtis (1872–1942) about the nature of nebulas. Today astronomers use the term nebula (which means "cloud" in Latin) to describe interstellar clouds of gas or dust, but before the advent of powerful telescopes, any fuzzy celestial object was described as a nebula. Some were clouds of dust, but Curtis held the view that others, known as spiral nebulas, lay outside our galaxy. One such was the Andromeda nebula, a spiral-shaped cluster known to western astronomers since the 17th century. Curtis estimated its distance from Earth to be about 500,000 light-years. He believed that spiral nebulas like Andromeda were independent star systems, something he described as "island universes," which were "comparable with our own galaxy in dimension and in number of component units." Shapley disagreed: he thought that spiral nebulas lay inside the galaxy.

STUDYING ANDROMEDA

In 1917 a powerful 100-inch (2.54-m) telescope came into operation at Mount Wilson Observatory, and in 1923 Hubble used this to make his first major astronomical discovery, perhaps the most

HENRIETTA LEAVITT 1868-1921

Henrietta Leavitt was born in Lancaster, Massachusetts, the daughter of a Congregational minister. After graduating in 1892 from Radcliffe College, in Cambridge, Massachusetts, she worked as a research assistant at the Harvard College Observatory, later becoming head of the observatory's department of photographic photometry. Her work involved studying the brightness (or magnitude) of stars as recorded on photographic plates. The photographic magnitude of a star differs from its visual magnitude as a photographic emulsion is more sensitive to blue light than the eye. In 1907 the director of the observatory, Edward Pickering (1846–1919), announced plans to redetermine stellar magnitudes by photographic techniques. Leavitt established a standard of photographic measurements of stars' magnitudes, accepted by the Inter national Committee on Photographic Magnitudes in 1913 and called the Harvard Standard. Pickering held attitudes typical of the time toward women, which meant that Leavitt was unable to pursue her own lines of inquiry but had to carry out work assigned by him. One of these tasks was to search for variable stars. During her career Leavitt discovered more than 2,400 of them, almost half the total then known. Her work on Cepheids led the way to their being used as "mileposts" for judging distances in space. Like astronomer Annie Jump Cannon (1863– 1941), a coworker at the Harvard Observatory, Leavitt was deaf. This may be why both women were so outstanding at meticulous observation: Cannon was later named the "census-taker of the sky." Leavitt was only in her mid-50s when she died of cancer in 1921; a colleague remembered her as "possessing the best mind at the observatory."

important of his career. He turned the telescope on Andromeda and succeeded in resolving the outer region of the nebula into "dense swarms of images which in no way differ from those of ordinary stars." He observed that there were a number of giant yellow Cepheid stars within the nebula. Using these as distance-markers, Hubble was able to calculate that Andromeda is about 1 million light-years distant (this figure was in fact an underestimate), and consequently far outside our galaxy. This was the first firm evidence confirming the existence of Curtis's "island universes."

Between 1925 and 1929 Hubble published three major papers showing that spiral nebulas are at enormous distances outside our galaxy—that they are in fact isolated systems of stars. Hubble's data

MILEPOSTS IN THE SKY

The relative brightness of stars is measured by their magnitude: the brighter the object, the lower its magnitude. A star of any one magnitude is approximately 2.51 times brighter than a star of the next magnitude; thus a star of magnitude 5 is 2.51 times as bright as a star of magnitude 6. Because a very bright, distant star may appear to us much dimmer than a nearer but fainter star, astronomers distinguish between how bright a star appears to us, its apparent magnitude, and how bright it really is, its absolute magnitude, calculated as the brightness it would have if viewed from a distance of 10 parsecs (32.6 light-years). If a star's absolute magnitude can be determined, it is then possible to calculate its distance from Earth.

Henrietta Leavitt (right) spent many years analyzing the photographic magnitudes of stars—their brightness as recorded on photographic plates. She noted there were many Cepheid variables, a particular type of star, within a body known as the Large Magellanic Cloud (LMC), a close neighbor of our own galaxy. Cepheid variables are named after the Cepheus constellation where they were first seen. They are known to vary in brightness over very precise and specific periods of time, from between 1 and 50 days. Leavitt observed that the brighter Cepheids had the longer periods of brightness, and by 1912 she was able to show that the apparent brightness of Cepheids decreased proportionately with the length of the period. From these observations, she was able to calculate a cycle–brightness ratio that could be applied to all Cepheid variables.

Danish astronomer Ejnar Hertzsprung (1873– 1967) took Leavitt's work on Cepheids a stage further. He realized that the cycle–brightness ratio she had established was related to the Cepheids' absolute magnitude. By observing the period of variation and brightness of Cepheid variables in any group of stars it would be possible to estimate the distance of that group from Earth. This was a very significant advance in astronomical science. Cepheid variables could now function as mileposts in the sky, allowing astronomers to calculate distances between stars and across far-off galaxies.

suggested that our galaxy is the largest in the universe. We know now that it is simply one among many—an average-size spiral galaxy. There are about 100 billion galaxies in the universe, each one of which contains about 300 billion stars.

ANOTHER DISCOVERY

As Hubble continued his exploration of these outer galaxies (or extra galactic nebulas, as he termed them), he went on to make a second major discovery. He found that they are apparently moving away from ours, and that the farther away they are, the faster they are moving away. Hubble was able to prove this by studying the "redshift" of various galaxies. "Redshift" is a phenomenon that is similar to the Doppler effect. The definition of this is "a change in a wavelength because of relative motion between the source of the wavelength and an observer." An everyday example is the noise made by the siren of a passing police car. If you are standing in the street, as the car approaches you will notice a rise in pitch, followed by a fall in pitch as the car passes you by.

This happens because sound travels in waves, and the frequency of the sound waves is linked to pitch. High frequency waves create a high-pitched sound, and low-frequency waves give out a low-pitched sound. As a sound-emitting object (the police car in this case) approaches, the sound waves become bunched together, shortening their wavelength and increasing

their frequency—and so increasing their pitch. As the object moves away, the waves spread out, resulting in a longer wavelength, a lower frequency, and so a lower pitch.

Light also travels in waves. The different frequencies of light waves correspond to different colors. At one end of the scale lower-frequency waves produce the color red; at the other end of the scale higher-frequency waves produce the color blue. Light waves moving toward us are compressed, have a higher frequency, and so shift toward the blue end of the scale. Light traveling away from an observer will spread out and have a lower frequency, so its wavelengths shift toward the red end of the scale.

The faster the light-emitting objects recede, the greater is the shift to red. By 1929 Hubble had noticed that the more distant the galaxy, the greater its redshift. That is how he came to his conclusion that galaxies are moving away from us. He then drew a graph of the relationship between the speed they are moving and their distance from Earth, and showed that their speed increases proportionately with their distance from us. A galaxy twice as far away will have twice the redshift, and a galaxy ten times farther away will have ten times the redshift. This is now known as Hubble's law.

Working with the 100-inch (2.54-m) telescope, and in collaboration with his colleague Milton Humason (1891–1972), Hubble examined many more galaxies between 1928 and 1936. He found that the relationship between distance and redshift always held true. But what did these redshifts mean? Scientists gradually began to believe that the reason galaxies are moving away from us is because the universe is expanding. What is happening is most easily explained by imagining dots drawn over a partially inflated balloon. These dots represent other galaxies. As the balloon is inflated further, so it expands, making the dots move even farther apart from one another.

STATIC OR EXPANDING?

The idea that the universe might be expanding was first put forward by theoretical physicists, scientists who base their theories of matter and energy on logical reasoning from known data. The greatest of early 20th century physicists, Albert Einstein (1879–1955), had described the universe as static ("matter with no motion"). In 1917, Dutch astronomer and mathematician Willem de Sitter (1872–1934) found a solution to the equations in Einstein's general theory of relativity that described an expanding universe ("motion with no matter"). Russian astronomer Aleksandr Friedmann (1888– 1925) announced similar findings in 1922.

In 1927 Belgian astronomer George Lemaître (1894–1966) also decided that the universe must be expanding. He believed it had begun as a "primal atom." There could well have been some instability at this point, he argued, producing the immense explosion that created the universe we see today. This later became known as the "big-bang" theory, though the name was not coined until 1950, by British astronomer Fred Hoyle (see box above). Today the big-bang theory is the most commonly accepted scientific model of how the universe had its beginnings. The model states that about 12 to 15 billion years ago the universe exploded from an extremely dense, hot state, and

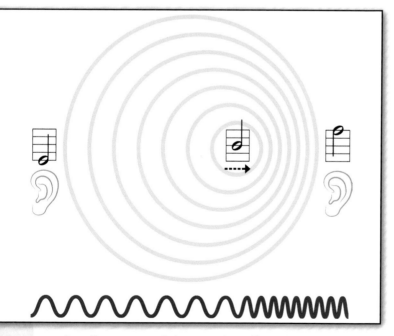

This illustration of the Doppler effect shows how wavelengths affect how we hear sounds that are moving toward us and away from us.

THE HUBBLE SPACE TELESCOPE

The Hubble Space Telescope (HST) is named for Edwin Hubble in recognition of his astronomical achievements. An Earth-orbiting telescope, it was developed by the National Aeronautics and Space Administration (NASA) in the United States between 1977 and 1985. The explosion of the Challenger space shuttle shortly after lift-off on January 28, 1986, which led to the suspension of all shuttle flights, delayed its launching from the space shuttle Discovery until 1990. The HST has a low orbit—it travels 965 miles (600 km) above the surface of the Earth—and it carries an astronomical telescope with a mirror 7.87 feet (2.4 m) in diameter. It also has a spectroscope that can study the light from objects at infrared, ultraviolet, and visible wavelengths. Several cameras and a microwave radio link to Earth complete the equipment, which is powered by electricity generated by "arrays" of solar panels. The telescope weighs 11 tons (9.98 tonnes), and is 43 feet (13 m) in length.

The first pictures from the HST were disappointing because of a flaw in the mirror, but its faults were corrected in a 1993 NASA shuttle mission. Since then the HST has produced stunning photographs of many celestial objects with a clarity that can be obtained because the telescope is situated above the interference and turbulence of the Earth's atmosphere. Not only have these photographs enabled astronomers to study the solar system in much greater detail than ever before, but they have provided unprecedented views of different types of stars and galaxies in outer space, including long sought-after failed stars known as brown dwarfs. The HST is expected to keep working until at least the year 2014 and possibly as long as 2020.

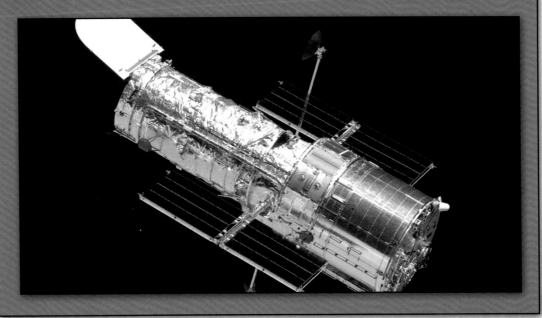

FRED HOYLE 1915–2001

Astronomer and mathematician Fred Hoyle was born in Bingley, Yorkshire, northern England, and studied at Cambridge University, where he was later professor of astronomy and experimental philosophy (1958–72). In 1948, with British cosmologist Hermann Bondi (1919–2005) and astronomer Thomas Gold (1920–2004), Hoyle proposed the "steady state" theory of the origin of the universe. This alternative model to the big-bang theory suggested that the universe had always existed in its present form and that new matter was constantly being created to sustain its density. Although this theory is no longer widely accepted, Hoyle went on to formulate other theories on the origins of stars and elements within them. From 1972–78, Hoyle was professor-at-large at Cornell University, in Ithaca, New York. He is the author of many books on scientific matters, including science fiction.

that as the expanding matter and radiation gradually cooled, stars and galaxies were formed.

Scientists have speculated that the universe will reach a limit of expansion, and will then begin to collapse, like a deflating balloon, until it reaches a very dense state again. It will then undergo another big bang. However, the most recent observations suggest that the expansion of the universe is getting faster and will never halt.

Although Hubble was regarded by many as the creator of the idea of the expanding universe, he did not completely support the notion himself. Expansion, he agreed, was one possible interpretation, but another theory, favored by Hubble, was that the redshift might be caused by "tired light." In the course of its journey from distant galaxies, Hubble argued, light would lose energy.

The frequency of its wavelength would diminish, and so its wavelength would lengthen. For this reason, by the time it reaches Earth, it would be significantly shifted toward the red. If Hubble were correct, the redshift could have nothing at all to do with the expansion of the universe.

CLASSIFYING GALAXIES

As a result of his observations at Mount Wilson, Hubble identified three types of galaxy by their shape—elliptical, spiral, and barred spiral. He then further divided these into a number of subtypes. Subsequently, types of galaxy have been found that do not fit into Hubble's scheme, but it is still widely used as the basis for classification.

Some astronomers used the different shapes of galaxy identified by Hubble to produce theories about the way that galaxies may have evolved, suggesting that ellipticals developed naturally into spirals (it is now thought that spirals merge to form ellipticals). Hubble himself was more cautious, stressing that "the basis of the classification is descriptive, and entirely independent of theory." Hubble's work with the great telescope

Edwin Hubble was a pioneer in extragalactic astronomy, which is the study of objects beyond our own galaxy, the Milky Way.

Edwin Hubble did not want a funeral and even today, the site of his burial is not known.

at Mount Wilson made him a public success, and he was often visited there by celebrities from Hollywood such as movie star Charlie Chaplin (1889–1977) and producer Walt Disney (1901–1966). He relished such attention, along with the opportunities for travel that his fame brought.

But prolonged absences and overseas tours did not impress his colleagues, and when the directorship of the laboratory became vacant in 1945, Hubble, the obvious choice, was passed over in favor of the lesser-known Ira Bowen (1898–1973). Hubble died at San Marino, California, on September 28, 1953.

SCIENTIFIC BACKGROUND

Before 1910

French astronomer Charles Messier (1730–1817) publishes the first catalog of nebulas and star clusters

Cepheids are first described by British astronomer John Goodricke (1764–1786)

Austrian physicist Christian Doppler (1803–1853) describes the Doppler effect

1910

1912–14 Hubble trains and works as a lawyer before returning to university to study astronomy

1912 American astronomer Henrietta Leavitt (1868–1921) works out a standard for photographic measurement of the magnitude of Cepheid stars

1915

1917 Hubble obtains his Ph.D. in astronomy

1919 Hubble starts work at Mount Wilson Observatory near Pasadena, California

1920

1920 American physicist Harlow Shapley (1885–1972) and astronomer Heber Curtis (1982–1942) debate the existence of "island universes"

1922–24 Hubble observes that not all nebulas are in our galaxy, and that Cepheids are outside the Milky Way

1925

1930

1927 Belgian astronomer George Lemaître (1894–1966) supports Hubble's theory of an expanding universe and argues the "primal atom" model, later known as the big-bang theory

1929 Hubble's law established

1931 American radio engineer Karl Jansky (1905–1950) detects radio interference coming from the stars

1935

1936 After years of studying the redshifts of different galaxies, Hubble publishes *The Realm of the Nebulae*

1939 Hubble receives the gold medal of the Royal Astronomical Society, London

1940

1945

1948 The Mount Palomar 200-inch Hale telescope is commissioned

1950

After 1950

1960 First quasar described by American astronomer Allan Sandage (1926–2010)

1967 British astronomer Jocelyn Bell (1943–) discovers the first pulsar

1990 The Hubble Space Telescope is launched

POLITICAL AND CULTURAL BACKGROUND

1912 The African National Congress (A.N.C.) is formed in Bloemfontein, South Africa, as the main party protecting the interests of the nonwhite population

1908 The Austrian artist Gustav Klimt (1862–1918), one of the painters influenced by Art Nouveau, produces his most famous painting, *The Kiss*

1916 The main naval engagement of World War I (1914–18) takes place between Britain and Germany near Jutland in the North Sea; it is a strategic victory for Britain

1916 In the United States Jeanette Rankin of Montana, a state in which women have the vote, becomes the first woman to be elected to the U.S. Congress

1920 British writer Agatha Christie (1890–1976) publishes the first short story to feature the fictional detective Hercule Poirot: *The Mysterious Affair at Styles*

1928 Influential Mexican composer Carlos Chávez (1899–1978) founds the Mexican Symphony Orchestra, and becomes director of the National Conservatory

1928 Albania becomes a kingdom under King Zog I. The country rapidly falls under the influence of Mussolini's fascist government

1935 The Gibson electric guitar—the first electro-acoustic guitar—is manufactured in the United States

1937 The Irish Free State is renamed Eire and draws up a new constitution

1942 Work is completed on the Grand Coulee Dam on the Columbia River in the state of Washington; it is the largest dam in the world

1939 World War II breaks out in Europe as Germany invades Poland

1946 A new style of modern jazz, dubbed "bebop," comes into fashion. It is refined by the American saxophone player Charlie Parker (1920–1955)

1950 In the United States the character Charlie Brown makes his first appearance in a comic strip by cartoonist Charles Schultz (1922– 2000)

achromatic lens A lens made in two parts from different types of glass in order to overcome chromatic aberration.

additive process The type of color mixing that occurs when colored lights are mixed. See also *primary colors of light*.

angle of incidence The angle between an incident ray and the normal to a mirror or to the surface of a block of transparent material.

angle of reflection The angle between the reflected ray and the normal to a mirror.

angle of refraction The angle between the refracted ray and the normal to the surface of a block of transparent material.

arc light A type of electric light produced by a bright high-voltage spark passing between electrodes made from carbon or metal.

center of curvature Imagine that a curved mirror is part of a sphere. The center of curvature is the center of that sphere.

chromatic aberration A lens defect in which colored fringes form around the edges of an image produced by the lens. It occurs because each of the component colors of white light is brought to a slightly different focus.

combustion Also called burning, a type of chemical reaction that is accompanied by the production of heat and, usually, light.

concave lens Also called a diverging lens, a type of lens that causes parallel rays of light to spread out (diverge) as if coming from a point (the focus) behind the lens. Its surfaces curve inward.

concave mirror Also called a converging mirror, a type of mirror that causes parallel rays of light to be reflected to a focus in front of the mirror. Its surface curves inward.

condenser In optics a pair of convex lenses (converging lenses) used to concentrate light and provide even illumination in an optical instrument such as a microscope or slide projector.

converging lens Another name for a convex lens.

converging mirror Another name for a concave mirror.

convex lens Also called a converging lens, a type of lens that causes parallel rays of light to converge to a point (the focus) in front of the lens. Its surfaces curve outward.

convex mirror Also called a diverging mirror, a type of mirror that causes parallel rays of light to spread out (diverge) after reflection so that they appear to come from a point (the focus) behind the mirror. Its surface curves outward.

dispersion The splitting of white light into the colors of the rainbow (a spectrum), for example, by a triangular prism. Raindrops cause dispersion in a rainbow.

diverging lens Another name for a concave lens.

diverging mirror Another name for a convex mirror.

eclipse See *lunar eclipse*; *solar eclipse*.

erect Describing an image produced by a lens or other optical system that is the right way up.

fiber optics The use of thin glass or plastic fibers to carry light or pulses of light, usually representing coded information.

fluorescent bulb Also called a fluorescent tube, an electric lamp consisting of a tube containing mercury vapor, with electrodes at each end. Electric current flowing between the electrodes makes the mercury vapor emit ultraviolet light. This strikes the lining of the tube, which is made from phosphor, a substance that gives off bright white light.

focal length The distance from the center of a lens or mirror to its focus.

focus The point at which parallel light rays are brought together by a convex lens or concave mirror, or from which rays appear to come with a concave lens or convex mirror. For a curved mirror the focus lies midway between the mirror and its center of curvature.

image A representation of an object produced by a lens or mirror.

incandescence The emission of light by an object that is heated to white heat.

incandescent lamp An electric bulb that has a filament (usually made of tungsten) in a glass globe containing traces of an inert gas such as argon. The electric current heats the filament to incandescence.

incident ray A ray of light that strikes a mirror or enters a lens or other optical system.

inversion The reversal top to bottom of the image produced by a lens or other optical system. The image is said to be inverted.

lateral inversion The reversal left to right of the image produced by a mirror or other optical system. The image is said to be laterally inverted.

laws of reflection of light
1. The angle of incidence equals the angle of reflection.
2. The incident ray, the normal, and the reflected ray all lie in the same plane.

laws of refraction of light
1. (also known as Snell's law) The sine of the angle of incidence divided by the sine of the angle of refraction is a constant (the refractive index).
2. The incident ray, the normal, and the refracted ray all lie in the same plane.

lens A piece of transparent material that, by refraction, changes the direction of light rays passing through it. See also *focus*.

lunar eclipse An eclipse of the Moon, occurring when the Earth's shadow (cast by the Sun) falls onto the Moon.

magnifying glass A convex lens (converging lens) used to produce an enlarged image of an object.

microscope An instrument that produces a magnified image of a small object.

mirage An optical phenomenon in which a layer of warm air above hot ground refracts light rays from a distant object so that it is seen as a nearby inverted image.

mirror A reflective surface that forms an image.

normal A line at right angles to a mirror or to the surface of a block of transparent material. Angles of reflection and refraction are measured with respect to the normal.

opaque Describing a substance that does not allow light to pass through it. It is the opposite of transparent.

pentaprism A five-sided prism used in the viewfinder of a single-lens reflex camera.

periscope An optical instrument consisting of a vertical tube with an angled mirror or prism at each end. It is used for looking over obstructions or for looking while remaining unobserved (as from a submarine).

photoelectric cell Also called a photocell, a current-producing device consisting of an element such as silicon that emits electrons when struck by light.

photosynthesis The process in which green plants use the energy of sunlight to convert carbon dioxide and water into sugars and oxygen.

plano-convex lens A lens that has one convex surface (curving outward) and one flat surface. It is a type of converging lens.

primary colors of light The colors red, blue, and green, which, when mixed, produce white by the additive process.

primary colors of paint The colors yellow, cyan, and magenta, which, when mixed, produce black by the subtractive process.

primary rainbow The main part of a rainbow, resulting from the dispersion of sunlight by raindrops. Its colors, from outermost to innermost, are red, orange, yellow, green, blue, indigo, and violet.

prism A usually triangular block of a transparent material that can split white light into the colors of the rainbow.

radius of curvature The distance from a curved mirror to its center of curvature.

real image An image produced by a lens, mirror, or optical system that can be put on a screen (unlike a virtual image).

reflected ray A ray of light that is reflected by a mirror.

reflecting telescope Also called a reflector, a type of telescope that uses one or more curved mirrors to form an image.

refracted ray A ray of light that is refracted as it passes from one transparent material into another.

refracting telescope Also called a refractor, a type of telescope that uses lenses to form an image.

refraction The bending of light rays as they pass from one transparent material into another.

refractive index A measure of the amount by which light is refracted when it passes from one transparent material into another. It equals the sine of the angle of incidence divided by the sine of the angle of refraction.

secondary colors of light The colors yellow, cyan, and magenta, produced by mixing the primary colors of light in pairs.

secondary colors of paint The colors red, blue, and green, produced by mixing the primary colors of paint in pairs.

secondary rainbow A faint rainbow sometimes seen outside (higher than) the bright primary rainbow. Its colors, from outermost to innermost, are violet, indigo, blue, green, yellow, orange, and red—the reverse order from those in the primary rainbow.

Snell's law The first of the laws of refraction of light.

solar eclipse An eclipse of the Sun, caused by the Moon passing between the Earth and the Sun.

solar panel 1. A device consisting of hundreds of photoelectric cells used, for example, to provide the electric power for space probes. 2. A thin tank containing water and painted black. It absorbs the Sun's radiation, which heats the water.

spectrum The band of colors produced when, for example, light passes through a prism.

subtractive process The type of color mixing that occurs when colored inks or paints are mixed. See *primary colors of paint.*

telescope An instrument that produces a magnified image of a distant object. See *reflecting telescope; refracting telescope.*

transparent Describing a material that allows light to pass through it (such as glass or clear plastic).

virtual image An image produced by a lens, mirror, or optical system that cannot be put on a screen (unlike a real image).

wavelength The distance between two successive locations where a wave is at its maximum intensity.

George Eastman House/International
    Museum of Photography and Film
900 East Avenue
Rochester, NY 14607
585-271-3361
Web site: http://www.eastmanhouse.org
This photography and film museum and
    archive is located in the former
    home of George Eastman, who
    founded the Eastman Kodak
    Company and is often called the
    father of modern photography.

Haleakala Observatories
30,000 Haleakala Highway
Kula, HI 96790
808-572-4459
Web site: http://www.ifa.hawaii.edu/hale-
    akalanew/observatories.shtml
This complex of observatories is located
    on the island of Maui on the summit
    of Haleakala. The site was chosen for
    its limited light pollution and dry,
    still air. The observatories are oper-
    ated by the University of Hawaii, the
    U.S. Air Force, and other groups.

Intrepid Sea, Air, and Space Museum
Pier 86
W. 46th Street and 12th Avenue
New York, NY 10036
212-245-0072
Web site: http://www.intrepidmuseum.
    org/
In 2012, the space shuttle Enterprise was
    moved to this museum, located on a
    World War II aircraft carrier. The
    Space Shuttle Pavilion features the
    shuttle, along with many exhibits on
    the history of the shuttle program.

Kennedy Space Center
State Road 405
Cape Canaveral, FL, 32899
312-867-5000
Web site: http://www.kennedyspacecen-
    ter.com/
Kennedy Space Center has been the
    launch site of manned US space
    shuttles since 1968. A visit to the
    space center includes the US
    Astronaut Hall of Fame, IMAX films,
    exhibits on the history of human
    space exploration, and a close-up
    experience with the space
    shuttle Atlantis.

Mount Wilson Observatory
Mount Wilson
Los Angeles, CA 91023
626-440-9016
Web site: http://www.mtwilson.edu/
This observatory, where Edwin Hubble
    spent much of his career, offers tours
    to the public, as well as a chance for
    visitors to look through the historic
    60-inch reflecting telescope.

Museum of the Moving Image
36-01 35th Avenue
Astoria, NY 11106
718-784-0077
Website: http://www.movingimage.us/
The Museum of the Moving Image cele-
    brates the history, artistic vision, and
    technology of film, television, and
    digital media. The core exhibition
    features over 1,400 artifacts related
    the moving images, from 19th
    century optical toys to today's
    video games.

Smithsonian National Air and Space
 Museum
Independence Avenue at 6th Street SW
Washington, DC 20560
202-633-2214
Web site: http://airandspace.si.edu/visit/
 mall/
This museum showcases the history of
 air and space exploration and fea-
 tures the Apollo 11 Command
 Module, the Albert Einstein
 Planetarium, an observatory open to
 the public, and much more.

Solar Energies Industries Association
505 9th Street NW
Suite 800
Washington, DC 20004
202-682-0556
Web site: www.seia.org
This trade association is made up of
 companies and groups that research
 solar energy and manufacture solar
 energy products.

WEB SITES

Due to the changing nature of Internet
links, Rosen Publishing has developed
an online list of Web sites related to the
subject of this book. This site is updated
regularly. Please use this link to access
the list:

http://www.rosenlinks.com/CORE/Light

Bortz, Fred. *The Big Bang Theory: Edwin Hubble and the Origins of the Universe*. Revolutionary Discoveries of Scientific Pioneers. New York: Rosen Publishing Group, 2014.

Brox, Jane. *Brilliant: The Evolution of Artificial Light*. New York: Houghton Mifflin Harcourt, 2010.

Changizi, Mark. *The Vision Revolution: How the Latest Research Overturns Everything We Thought We Knew About Human Vision*. Dallas, TX: BenBella Books, 2011.

Dickinson, Terence. *Hubble's Universe: Greatest Discoveries and Latest Images*. Richmond Hill, Ontario: Firefly Books, 2013.

Dickinson, Terence. *NightWatch: A Practical Guide to Viewing the Universe*. Richmond Hill, Ontario: Firefly Books, 2007.

English, Neil. *Choosing and Using a Refracting Telescope*. New York: Springer Publishing Company, 2011.

English, Neil. *The Science and Art of Using Telescopes*. New York: Springer Publishing Company, 2010.

Feynman, Richard P. *QED: the Strange Theory of Light and Matter*. Princeton, NJ: Princeton University Press, 2006.

Fowles, Grant R. *Introduction to Modern Optics*. Mineola, NY: Dover Publications, 2012.

Gibilisco, Stan. *Optics Demystified*. New York: McGraw-Hill Professional, 2010.

Gribbin, John. *Galaxies: A Very Short Introduction*. Oxford, UK: Oxford University Press, 2008.

Harrington, Philip S. *Star Ware: The Amateur Astronomer's Guide to Choosing, Buying, and Using Telescopes and Accessories*. Hoboken, NJ: Wiley Publishing, 2011.

Houston, Rick. *Wheels Stop: The Tragedies and Triumphs of the Space Shuttle Program, 1986–2011*. Lincoln, NE: University of Nebraska Press, 2014.

Johnson, B.K. *Optics and Optical Instruments: An Introduction*. Mineola, NY: Dover Publications, 2013.

Milonni, Peter W., and Joseph H. Eberly. *Laser Physics*. Hoboken, NJ: Wiley Publishing, 2010.

Rappaport, Helen, and Roger Watson. *Capturing the Light: The Birth of Photography, a True Story of Genius and Rivalry*. New York: St. Martin's Press, 2014.

Scott, Elaine. *Space, Stars, and the Beginning of Time: What the Hubble Telescope Saw*. New York: Clarion Books, 2011.

Tilley, Richard. *Colour and the Optical Properties of Materials: An Exploration of the Relationship Between Light, the Optical Properties of Materials and Colour*. Hoboken, NJ: Wiley Publishing, 2011.

R

radiation, 6, 12–13, 24, 54, 68, 78
radius, 26, 28, 86
rainbow, 16, 40, 44, 46
real image, 24
rectangular blocks, 22, 48
red, 6, 36, 42, 44, 52
redshift, 75–76, 79
reflected, 16– 20, 25–26, 32, 38, 40, 44–46, 60, 64, 66, 68
refracted, 30, 32, 34, 36, 46, 48, 50
relationship, 76
retina, 55
roofs, 12
rotation, 22
ruby, 68

S

scattered, 24
screen, 25, 42, 62, 65–66, 68
secondary colors, 42–44
semimetallic, 11
shadow(s), 14, 16
sharp image, 52
sheen, 64, 67
shooters, 58
shortsighted, 48, 54
shutter, 56, 62
signals, 34, 90
silicon, 10, 86
size, 28, 50, 54, 56, 70, 74
slide, 58, 60, 62
sodium, 40
space probe, 10
spark, 6–7
speed of light, 4, 18, 20, 22, 34
sphere, 16, 26
spoon, 26
stimulates, 67–68
straw, 30, 32

streetlights, 10, 40
submarines, 26
substances, 11, 14
sugar, 10
Sun, 10, 14, 16, 20, 24, 36
sunlight, 10, 36, 66
surfaces, 13, 16, 30–33, 48, 56, 67, 77
Swan, Joseph, 7
swarms, 75

T

tablespoon, 28
tall, 26
tears, 54
telephone, 34
telephoto, 56, 58
television, 42
theaters, 42
theory, 17, 76, 79–80
transparent, 30, 42, 54
travel, 14, 16–17, 19–22, 30–33, 64–66, 70–71, 75, 77, 80
troughs, 64–65
trucks, 40
tube, 6, 8, 58, 60–61, 68

U

United States, 4, 6, 76
universe 18, 70–72, 75–76, 78–79

V

vacuum, 6, 22, 64, 70
value, 20, 30, 32
vapor, 6, 8
vehicles, 29, 41
violet, 36, 44, 46, 66
virtual, 24, 28
vitreous, 54

PHOTO CREDITS